Growing Up Giffin

Growing Up Giffin

REFLECTIONS ON A HAPPY STEELTOWN BOYHOOD

Tim Hayes

With a Foreword by Robert Fragasso

The events, people, and places herein are depicted to the best recollection of the author, who assumes complete and sole responsibility for the accuracy of this narrative.

ISBN-13: 9781544955988
ISBN-10: 1544955987

To Kelsey, Jenna, and Chris,
who arrived later
but who have always shown
a brighter path ahead.

Contents

Acknowledgments

We arrive alone, and we leave alone. That's what the old saying tells us, and I suppose that's true.

But all the days in between those moments? Wow, are they filled with people who make life interesting, enthralling, infuriating, exciting, joyful, hopeful, beautiful, and a thousand other emotions!

In this collection of remembrances of my years growing up on a tightly packed, tightly knit middle-class street in the 1960s and '70s, I've had the pleasure of conjuring up so many of those faces, voices, and stories that had been quietly sleeping in some far-off corner of my consciousness. Some of the more obvious ones include my family, parents Pat and Marlene Hayes, and sisters Chris (Hayes) Nolin and Lori (Hayes) Williams.

Others include neighbors up and down both sides of our street. Can't forget Nick and Fran, the older couple who ran the neighborhood store, which doubled as a hangout spot and polling place.

Up at St. Joseph Roman Catholic Church and School, the leading lights included the pastor, Father Kraus, and school principal, Sister Frederick, along with some of my teachers during the eight years spent there: Sister Dorothy, Miss Katz, Mrs. Gardille, Sister Joachim, Mrs. Falkowski, Sister Ruth Ann, Sister James Ann, Sister Esther, and Mrs. Stupar. My apologies for any names forgotten along the way. Best buddies at St. Joe's included Bill, Dale, and Carl. Enemies—or, at least, the guys I was afraid of—well, I guess I'm still worried that you might still be on the loose and not yet incarcerated, so no names (not even first names) will be referenced here.

At Carrick High School, no listing would be complete without my favorite teacher there, Mr. Burleson, the band director and the adult who got to know and understand me better than anybody else in that enormous building, and who still has my utmost respect. Special kudos to Mr. Price, Mr. Cooper, Mr. Schwab, Mr. Mateka, and the lady who pushed me to realize my talent and love of writing, the faculty sponsor of *The Carrickulum* (get it?), our school newspaper, Mrs. Homburg. My best friends were those fellow members of the band, led by Bill (a different Bill, not the same as the one in grade school), Annette, Merita, Kim, Patty, Kevin, Ray, and Don. Thanks, you guys, for memories that still make me smile all these years later.

Someday I, just like everybody else in history, will leave this world, alone. But before that day arrives, I'm glad I got to live and learn and love alongside all of these folks. Growing Up Giffin, as you're about to read, was an absolute blast.

Foreword

Writing this foreword stirs memories and makes thoughtful connections to today. I hope that you, the reader, will see the same.

Tim Hayes is an accomplished writer, but even more so, he is a national award-winning speechwriter. As part of his craft, he must present the essence of an idea in a way that lets readers and listeners see the core of the message quickly and clearly. Tim's modus of collecting his blogs here is completely in that genre. He has taken us back to his and, by comparison, our youth to remember, and compare, what we are seeing in our lives today. How far we and the country have come will be evident, and so will the evolutionary connectivity of that time flow.

Tim sets his writings in the geographic location of his upbringing, an area within and adjacent to the city of Pittsburgh, Pennsylvania, called Mount Oliver. That borough and another section known as Knoxville are really the same neighborhood, bordering on each side of the central thoroughfare, Brownsville Road. This is mentioned because Brownsville Road begins in the heart of steelmaking territory, Pittsburgh's South Side with its fabled Jones & Laughlin steel works. The portraits of Messrs. Jones and Laughlin hang in the storied Duquesne Club, the club serving the elite of Pittsburgh since 1882. This is Pittsburgh's story and that of the country.

That connection to the mills and their founders is important because the area surrounding the South Side factories of J&L and similar steelmaking companies spawned the Mount Oliver area of which Tim writes. Originally Mount Oliver began at the end of the 19th century as the home for supervisors working in Pittsburgh's mills and allied smokestack industries. That was because Mount Oliver sat high above the Monongahela River, where the mills spewed out black smoke and particular debris that did not always reach to the heights above. So Mount Oliver housed the top strata of mill supervisors, and the names on the borough's buildings reflect the mostly German-American nature of its original population.

Brownsville Road represented the literal and figurative path from the hard life of the mills to the more quasi-suburban nature of Mount Oliver and then continued on toward the true suburbs of Brentwood, Whitehall, and the rural nature of Jefferson Hills. So it stood for the path toward a better, cleaner, and more prosperous life for Pittsburgh's working class.

By World War II, Pittsburgh's population had grown and become very dense on the prosperity of furnishing the war effort with crucial material and finished products for the military. After the war, Pittsburgh supplied the steel for domestic and international reconstruction and President Eisenhower's new national highway system.

We prospered, and those fathers returning from the war worked hard to send their sons and daughters to college and for specialized training so that they could have a better life and travel further on out Brownsville Road—once again, literally and figuratively.

But then a tragic momentum began to build for Pittsburgh and the entire industrial heartland of America. We rebuilt Europe and Asia, and they then had more modern and efficient mills than we and were using less-expensive labor, so they began to take away our business.

Political, business, and labor leaders were slow in recognizing this, intent on their respective pieces of the economic pie and not the entire mosaic, so we lost prominence. An economic tsunami hit with the oil embargo of 1973 and skyrocketing energy prices, meaning that our mills became even more unprofitable. They eventually shuttered, and we all know "the rest of the story," as a popular newscaster of the era would say. Tim's growing up spanned this wrenching transitional period.

Yet the work and family values of that World War II generation persisted, and Tim's generation was brought up on that and the feeling that everyone was in this together. Neighbors looked out for each other, and children still strove to achieve higher than had their parents.

It is Mount Oliver's story and it is America's story.

That story certainly isn't over, and we can gain great contemplative insight into today and tomorrow by reading Tim's compilation of his upbringing in Pittsburgh's Mount Oliver and America's heartland in an era of values and striving. He does it with humor, pathos, and the skills of the accomplished storyteller. Enjoy the read and the insight gained.

Robert Fragasso
Chairman and Chief Executive Officer,
Fragasso Financial Advisors

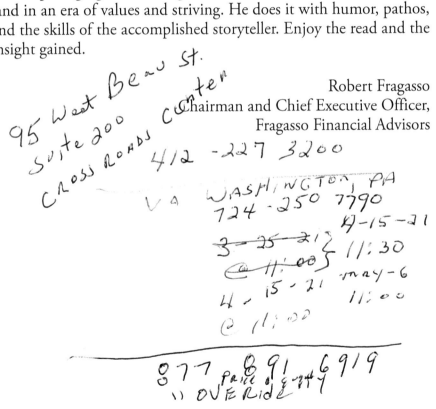

Introduction

At midlife a male in this society is supposed to be thinking of how to stay young, and I guess this book represents my typically off-kilter attempt at doing just that. But instead of looking for a girlfriend or a Corvette—neither of which I want or could afford anyway—I tell stories about what it was like growing up when and where and with whom I did.

Television's old Biography Channel had a tagline that reminded viewers, "Every life tells a story." That happens to be true, but most folks find themselves too busy actually living their lives to stop and recount the wonderful, scary, amazing, hysterically funny stories they're racking up along the way.

As a professional writer, I get paid to tell other people's stories. It's a great way to make a living, especially for someone like me who has always loved to write. Telling stories like the ones in this book, from a first-person perspective, has been exponentially easier, more revealing, and a hell of a lot more fun. Each of the essays here first appeared as an online blog, sent out each Sunday morning without fail to a distribution list of more than three hundred people: clients, friends, family, prospects, and people I've met in the course of conducting business at my communications practice, Tim Hayes Consulting (legal name: Transverse Park Productions LLC, by the way).

Looking back on people and events from a youth spent inside a loving, intact, strong, and wonderful family—one that included a rather sprawling extended family of aunts, uncles, grandparents, and cousins—along with eight years attending a smallish Catholic elementary school, with all the idiosyncrasies and quirks you might expect, and capping it off with four years at an gigantic public high school, where the full spectrum of economic, racial, and intellectual diversity came alive quickly and ferociously, this collection of stories only begins to plumb the possibilities.

But you have to start somewhere, and you're holding the result.

Our house sat squarely at the halfway point of the 500 block, the block at the very bottom of Giffin Avenue, in the borough of Mount Oliver, Pennsylvania, a self-sustaining municipality surrounded on all sides by another municipality, the city of Pittsburgh. Residents of Mount Oliver had to complete two tax local forms every year, one to pay the borough and one to pay the Pittsburgh Public Schools. Don't ask.

The borough was named in honor of Oliver Ormsby, the son of the original landowner, John Ormsby, for whom one of the main streets, Ormsby Avenue, also was named. Mount Oliver, back in the day, featured some of the greatest attractions for locals, and especially kids. For those of us living on Giffin Avenue, we had it made. A neighborhood store, owned, operated, and lived in by a colorful Italian husband and wife, offered penny candy, Push-Ups (flavored ice in a plastic tube), individual bottles of Pepsi in a slide-top cooler, and a pinball machine that you could play all day if you wanted and had enough quarters.

The houses along Giffin stood no more than ten feet apart from one another, but we never felt cramped. Cyclone fences separated the backyards, which stepped down about five feet from one house to the next, as the street slanted down a hill. We all knew everybody else's business, but we all hung together as true neighbors, too—never more so than when tragedy would strike and the people of Giffin would rush to a neighbor's aid.

We made our own fun, with "coming home when the streetlights came on" standing as one of the very few rules we had to follow. All that my friends and I had to do to start a day's adventure was run across Giffin Avenue, through a neighbor's backyard, and down a well-worn hillside dirt path to reach one of the centerpieces of our lives: Transverse Park. Complete with swings, slides, a pool, basketball courts, baseball diamonds, a football field, and a maintenance building chockablock with board games and other activities, the park drew us like a giant crabgrass magnet. I hold the significance of that place so deeply in my mind and heart that I named my company after it.

My fellow kids on the block attended either Mount Oliver Elementary or St. Joseph School. I went to St. Joe's, as did my two younger sisters behind me. Filled with a mixture of nuns—some cool, most not—and lay teachers—some okay, others certifiably nuts— and administered under the watchful, strict, yet secretly benevolent gaze of Sister Frederick, St. Joe's gave us eight years of top-notch education, consistent faith formation, and the occasional emotional trauma.

Just about everybody on Giffin then attended Carrick High School, part of the Pittsburgh Public Schools system. At Carrick, the protected, sheltered, limited shell built after eight years in Catholic school got shattered, which I believe had been a good thing—once the shock wore off. In high school, I made some of my closest friends, learned how to be a better friend, and got my first real taste of journalistic writing and newspaper production, setting me on my ultimate career path as a writer.

People look at me as if I've gone off the rails when I tell them I loved growing up, in all of the phases and places that the experience entailed. Nonetheless, it's true. Even the weird episodes, or the ones that left scars. It all adds up to the person you eventually turn out to be, and I wouldn't want to alter a single bit of it.

Truth be told, Mount Oliver in the decades since I laid my head there has seen some hard, rocky times. As my generational peers grew up, they left and didn't come back—myself included. In time, my parents moved out of our home on Giffin Avenue.

Occasionally, as part of meeting and working with clients today, I'll find myself in the general vicinity of Mount Oliver and take a quick spin down Giffin, past the old neighborhood store, even up to St. Joe's. Why I do this remains a mystery, because it stirs up happy memories as well as a crushing sense of loss at what's happened to all of my boyhood touchstone landmarks.

I suppose I'm looking, hoping, betting that my old house will have been spruced up, with a clean, clipped lawn and a fresh coat of paint on those metal awnings …

… or that there will be a group of kids hanging out in front of the store again, instead of a dark, empty building staring back at me …

… or that I'll see and hear hundreds of elementary school pupils in dress slacks and skirts running around and playing tag on an uneven asphalt playground at lunchtime, not a tattered handful of school buildings, standing as silent sentries to a once-vibrant parish school that couldn't survive long term.

But for as much as a sentimentalist as I might be, I'm also a realist. I also believe that communities such as Mount Oliver can come back. It first takes a belief, quickly followed by focused, attainable action that drives progress forward. It's long past the time to do my part for the little patch of Americana that's meant so much to me. That is why a percentage of the proceeds from the sale of this book will be donated to economic development efforts working to bring Mount Oliver fully back to the wonderful, happy, secure, economically thriving community of neighbors that I remember. Your support, in purchasing this book, is very much appreciated.

I loved Growing Up Giffin. And I hope you enjoy recounting some of the highlights along the way in this collection.

GIFFIN AVENUE:
My Favorite Oasis of Faces and Places

Here's what you would call the best of all possible worlds: growing up safe, provided for, and loved, while at the same time being too young to realize how badly the world was spinning into anarchy in the 1960s and early '70s. That sums up life for a boy with a David Letterman-sized gap between his two front teeth, jet black hair, and a penchant for words, even as a scrawny little kid.

Betcha by Golly, Wow

B ack in the day, long before music got downloaded from a computer and billed to a credit card, back when a weirdly shaped chip of plastic snapped into the big hole in the middle of a 45-rpm record so that you could play it on your family's stereo, getting your hands on—and your ears around—a favorite song took a little bit of work.

In my little hometown, that meant scraping up the dollar or so it would take to buy the record, hoofing it to the three-block-long business district almost a mile from our front door, and stepping right into my favorite store: the Mount Oliver Record Shop.

The store couldn't have been more than twenty feet wide, but it went back pretty far, with rack after rack of records—vinyl records that you listened to with a needle riding the groove of each song, decades before vinyl suddenly became cool again. Albums and album covers lined the walls above the racks of stereophonic merchandise. For a kid who loved listening to the radio, and *American Top 40* in particular, you couldn't beat spending as much time as possible in the record shop.

Too bad the old guy who owned it didn't feel the same way. He made it look as if every second spent in the place caused him untold pain and irritation. It took awhile to get used to seeing an angry old guy with hair coming out of his ears, standing behind the cash register giving you dirty looks, when next to him stood the coolest of the record shop's prized attractions: a stack of tiny brochures from 13Q, the city's leading bubblegum music station.

Those 13Q brochures came out fresh each week, with a picture of a deejay, the Top 10 songs for the week, lyrics to one of the most popular songs, and a lot of Peter Max-type artwork. If I got a hold of one of those 13Q brochures today, I'm sure it would look like absolute garbage, but back then? They were like gold. And the grumpy-puss running the store treated them like gold, too. He used to try to force kids to buy a record before he'd let them take a brochure, but when you summoned enough guts to call him on it, he'd let you slide, even as he narrowed his eyes and tried to make you feel like a crook in the process.

One sunny 1972 Saturday morning, I walked down to the record shop to buy a 45 that I really liked. New record and 13Q brochure in hand, I couldn't wait to get back home and flip it onto the record player. On the way back to my house stood the little family-owned corner neighborhood store (years before 7-Eleven or anything like that came along), where some of the older, tougher kids would hang out, playing pinball and generally getting up to no good.

One of these local hoods—let's call him Brick—carried some extra pounds and had a reputation for pushing around younger, scrawnier kids like me for fun. He had an Achilles' heel, though. In the corner of his left eye, a strange greenish mark stood out. It never went away. Nobody ever told me what it was or how it got there, and I sure as hell was never going to ask.

But the goofy green mark wasn't what got to old Brick. The thing that would set him off, vowing to pummel anyone stupid enough to do this, was starting to sing the old Sugarloaf single "Green-Eyed Lady." He would go absolutely berserk, sort of like the Hulk in the comic books. What is it about the color green and anger issues?

Anyway, I had to walk past the store on my way home with my new 45 when Brick shouted, "Hey! Whatcha got there, you little jerk?"

"I bought a new record."

"Oh, well, let's see it! Give it here!"

And as Brick snatched the paper bag out of my hand, he pulled out the record, paused for a second, and then started laughing his head off.

"What the hell kind of stupid song is this? 'Betcha by Golly, Wow'? Haw-haw! What are you, some kinda dumbbell? That's the dumbest name of a song I ever heard of! Haw-haw!"

Then he started tossing the record around like a Frisbee to the other juvenile delinquents hanging around the store, all of them laughing as I jumped and lurched, trying to intercept it without it breaking into a hundred pieces.

Then it happened.

Some brave—or was it foolish—kid came walking down the other side of the street, saw all the commotion, and began warbling, "Green-eyed lady, lovely laaa-deeee!" Brick snapped his enraged head in the offender's direction, threw my 45 back at me, and took off, threatening to kill that kid in short order.

I tore home in the opposite direction, ran straight to the record player, and started enjoying my new purchase, the 13Q brochure from the record shop safely ensconced in the pocket of my Sears blue jeans.

It's probably a good thing I didn't encounter Brick after my next venture to the record store, when I bought "Rockin' Pneumonia and the Boogie-Woogie Flu." I might have never gotten that one back.

Ten-Speeds to South Park

It had to be one of those cosmic coincidences. Somehow that December, the planets aligned in just the right sequence, and the gods of parental Christmas gift decisions decided to blow our collective preteen minds.

My best friends in the neighborhood and I all found new ten-speed bicycles next to our respective Christmas trees that year. Far out! We felt luckier than Greg Brady, Keith Partridge, and Donny Osmond put together.

The ten-speed bike in those years stood unchallenged as the coolest piece of equipment a thirteen-year-old boy could own. You'd never in a million years use all ten speeds, but that wasn't the point. The point was that you had ten speeds under your command, right at your fingertips. Combine that with the racing handlebars and silver shiny hand brakes, and you immediately became the Evel Knievel of your block. Untouchable. Irrefutable. You basked in ten speeds of neighborhood glory.

So, once the warm weather returned, all of us cool dudes decided there was only one thing to do with our new, un-road-tested ten-speeds. We needed to pedal out to South Park.

Now, South Park stood about fifteen miles from our neighborhood, over some of the hilliest roadways of Pittsburgh. None of us had ever ridden a bike anywhere near fifteen miles at a stretch, certainly never through city traffic, and absolutely not up and down the steep slopes between home and South Park.

But we had ten-speeds, man. We had the hardware, baby. Evel would do it. So we were riding to South Park, doubters be damned.

I'm here to tell you that we made it that day. It took hours. It took everything we had. It took sweat and tears, but no blood, thank goodness. We rode past the giant sign reading South Park, rolled our ten-speeds onto the grass, and collapsed, exhausted, totally spent.

It's human nature, I suppose, to want to make the most out of new toys. For my buddies and me, it took the form of riding our new ten-speed bikes to an outrageously inappropriate destination. When you grow up, it can be making every slide on a PowerPoint presentation spin or fade in or rotate or bounce, because you can. Or shoehorn use of a new technology into business practices or classroom curriculum for no good reason, just because it's there.

I served as a judge of a college public-relations class competition a couple of years ago and was equal parts appalled and amused because virtually every PR campaign cooked up by the students pivoted on heavy use of Facebook and Twitter. This included a campaign promoting increased applications for an assisted-living facility for senior citizens. Not sure Grandma and Grandpa live by the Tweet, kids.

Just because you have a shiny new toy doesn't mean it should become the be-all, end-all option for every possible application. That's all I'm saying.

My sweaty, exhausted friends and I learned that lesson in no uncertain terms one very long, very hot and sunny day during my thirteenth year. Yeah, our ten-speeds got us the fifteen hilly miles to South Park. But after we found a pay phone, our dads had to come out and drive us, and our bikes, back home.

A Very Transverse Fourth

"Do they have the Fourth of July in England?" asked Sister Joachim, my fourth-grade teacher. My hand shot up instantly. "Mr. Hayes?"

"Yes, they do. It's the day after the third of July," I proudly proclaimed, refusing to fall for the crafty nun's trick question and earning the snide sneers of my fellow pint-sized Catholics.

Ah, the Fourth of July. Summer's unofficial halftime celebration. Uniquely American, held under the broiling sun, with family and friends and barbecues and fireworks. You gotta love the Fourth of July.

Where I grew up, we loved it even more because the tiny municipality where we lived blew damn near its entire civic recreational budget each year putting on an all-day and well-past-nightfall celebration. My buddies and I couldn't get enough of it.

We'd head down to Transverse Park—right over the hill from my house, and the place where I spent most of my childhood, other than school and bed—as early as possible to help the grown-ups set up a row of about twenty wooden booths out near the left-field line of the baseball diamond.

Most of the booths hosted games of chance, such as throwing darts at balloons, the fish pond, ring toss over empty Pepsi bottles, and plenty more. The rest served up hot dogs, hot sausage sandwiches, hamburgers, penny candy, all the good stuff.

And the best part? As we helped set up the booths, we'd get a quarter here, a buck or two there, providing most of the dough we'd need later to play the games and eat the grub. Oh, it was awesome. Practicing capitalism on the Fourth of July! How American can you get?

My grandma lived about two blocks from the park on the other side, so just as the sun would start to bake the grass and dirt to a toasty temperature around lunchtime, we would head over there and get in on the big family get-together. My dad and uncles would be sitting in the shade, sipping cans of Iron City, listening to the Pittsburgh Pirates game on the radio, and keeping an eye on the coals in the hibachi. (Yes, I know. We were eating down at the park, also. But when you're nine, you can eat your weight in burgers and hot dogs and never feel a thing.)

After lunch at Grandma's, all my guy cousins would join us back at the park to watch the annual donkey baseball game (yes, it's grown men playing baseball on the backs of actual live donkeys—don't ask, but it was hilarious), the Little League championship game, a concert by a local band on a separate stage, and, of course, more chances to win and eat at the booths.

As evening approached, the party at Grandma's broke up and we all headed back to our houses to rest up for the main attraction: fireworks! Our strategy, perfected after years of observation and adjustment, included getting to the far end of the park and planting ourselves long before dusk, just as the firemen began stringing the rope to keep spectators safe. Our noses came right up to that rope, so we had front-row seats to all the action.

While people waited for the sky to become dark enough to start the show, the firemen entertained us with a battle to see which team could propel a barrel on an elevated line to the other side using fire hoses. If anybody's house actually caught fire on the Fourth of July, he would be good and truly screwed because the entire brigade was otherwise occupied at the park.

The fireworks seemed to get bigger and better each year, but we had even more to see than the stuff up in the sky; we had "groundworks," too, special pyrotechnic features set up at eye level. When the groundworks lit up the name of our town (MT OLIVER) in five-foot letters, that became the cue for the grand finale to begin.

Excited, exhausted, stomachs extended, we'd head home to collapse into bed as another Fourth would come to a close. But come the dawn, we'd be down the park again, carefully combing acre upon acre of grass, picking up all the loose change dropped by revelers the day before.

I mean, how American can you get? You gotta love the Fourth of July. And for us, the fifth wasn't all that bad, either.

Art Appreciation

Art carried all the keys down at Transverse Park.

He was a good man to get to know. Art could unlock the basketballs, the checkerboards, or the shuffleboard pucks and sticks. He could repair the seesaw or sliding board. He could even turn on the sprinklers at the pool anytime he wanted.

Transverse Park stood about a hundred yards from my house as a kid. My friends and I would tear out of our back doors after school or the first thing on Saturday morning, yell "Down the park!" to let our moms know where we were headed, run through a neighbor's yard on the other side of the street, skid down a well-worn hillside path, and get to the park for hours of unstructured, totally self-directed outdoor fun. No parents, carpools, uniforms, or trophies required. A wonderful way to grow up, and something most kids today couldn't even begin to fathom.

Art always struck me as a pretty old guy, but as I remember him now, he probably wasn't all that old. Maybe in his late fifties or early sixties. But whatever his age, he looked older than that number.

I have no idea what his backstory truly encompassed, of course, being a kid myself at the time. My assumption, though, held that Art had lived sort of a rough life. Perhaps working as a laborer in the steel mills, which back in the early 1970s were still roaring away.

Art always looked tired. He moved pretty slowly. He never seemed as if he had two nickels to rub together. He sighed a lot, watching each day drift by. A lonesome sort of sadness enveloped him. The energy required to unlock a cinder block shed full of sporting equipment for neighborhood kids most likely suited Art just fine at that point in his life.

And it wasn't anything like the creepy-scoutmaster-who-always-seemed-like-such-a-nice-man sort of thing we hear about almost daily in the news today. Art was harmless to all of us kids. To the extent he was capable of it, I think he got a kick out of working at the park. We were never in any danger from Art. Plus, the houses in our neighborhood were built practically on top of one another, so if anything untoward ever happened, every parent on the block would know and it would stop immediately.

During the summer, as we played baseball or rode the swings or played tag, around 7 p.m. we'd surreptitiously listen for the telltale ding!-ding! of the Goodie Bar truck to pull up curbside at the park. Armed with a quarter or two, we'd get our snow cones and ice Push-Ups, taking a break from the action to enjoy a tasty treat.

We never saw Art purchase anything from the Goodie Bar guy, though. One balmy and humid evening, a bunch of us chipped in and bought Art a grape snow cone. We took it over to him as he sat on a little wooden folding chair outside his equipment shed. You'd have thought we had given him a gold watch.

He really didn't say much. Just nodded his head and accepted the gift. He might have even teased a hint of a smile along one corner of his mouth. We ran off and dove back into whatever game we'd been playing, never giving it another thought.

I'm not sure which happened first, whether I got to be too old to run "down the park" any longer or whether Art stopped working there. Either way, that chapter had closed. But thinking back now, I hope Art remembered that grape snow cone as the thank-you a bunch of kids meant it to be one hot summer's evening.

He was a good guy to get to know.

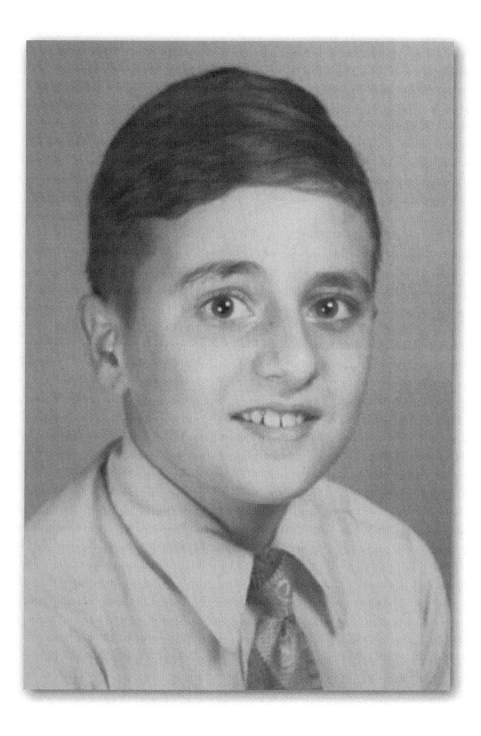

Baked Potato

So it wasn't exactly Tom Sawyer and his gang. We never faked our own deaths, explored in mysterious caves, or floated down a river on a raft. But we did bake some potatoes. Sort of.

Right behind the houses across the street from mine stood a field. A miracle of a field. Flat, level, with two enormous oak trees that stood the perfect distance apart to serve as the goal lines for two-hand touch football. The young male marauders of our neighborhood spent most of our summers on or around that field. The wind got knocked out of me for the first time on that field. I learned that I could kick a football farther than I could throw one on that field. We loved that field.

But you can play only so much football when you're eleven before your attention span darts away.

So one sweltering afternoon, one of the guys pipes up with a bright idea. "Let's make a fire pit and bake potatoes," he says.

"Yeah, let's do it!" we all affirmed, thereby cementing our reputation as cement-heads. Why, you might be asking, on a ninety-five-degree July day, would anybody want to light an open fire to bake and eat scalding-hot potatoes in a field?

Because of the adventure behind it, that's why. Duh.

We divvied up the assignments to pull off this stunt. One guy had to find bricks to make a circle around the fire pit. (We did have enough sense to avoid burning down our field; you have to give us that much credit.) One guy had to find sticks to make the fire, another to sneak out a roll of aluminum foil from home to wrap around the potatoes, another to get matches, another to get lighter fluid, and each of us had to go home and pilfer a raw potato from our mother's kitchen.

In those days, most of our moms stayed home during the day, adding a layer of cunning and creativity in our quixotic quest to bake these potatoes. Yet somehow it all came together thirty minutes later back on our field.

We picked our spot for the fire, ripped out enough grass to make a circle of dirt, laid the bricks around the edge, positioned the sticks in the middle, wrapped foil around the spuds, and waited for the magic to begin.

The kid in charge of aluminum acquisition faulted at his post a bit, meaning that a couple of the potatoes would have to go into our backyard barbecue buck naked. Let's just say this guy would never make quartermaster on a submarine. But this thing had elevated itself from a half-baked idea into the chance to half-bake some potatoes, and such sacrifices had to be made.

Lighter Fluid Guy dumped enough of the stuff on those sticks to launch the space shuttle. Matches Guy struck one, tossed it onto the pit, and we all came *this* close to becoming preadolescent flambé before the fire receded enough to drop our potatoes on top and await the culinary delights sure to result.

When you're eleven, the concept of time hasn't quite developed fully just yet. Also, you don't really have a good grasp of the difference between baking and roasting. What that translated to for us that amazingly hot day, after giving our midafternoon meal about ten minutes on that fire—remember, we had the attention span of a rock—were potatoes too hot to hold yet too raw to eat. Naturally, nobody thought of plates or forks, much less butter, salt, or sour cream.

So we spit out the lousy stuff, tossed the uneaten potatoes into the nearby woods (actually, I might have kicked mine, for greater distance), threw dirt on the fire (we had a couple of Cub Scouts who knew that stuff), and started a new football game.

I'm not sure, but probably a half hour later we got bored again and started some other ridiculous venture. Maybe whitewashing a fence.

Sharing Sullivan

M ore than fifty years ago, on a Sunday evening in February, Ed Sullivan, with his famously awkward arm-swooping motion, introduced the Beatles to the American television audience and changed the world.

Check the clip on YouTube. It's utterly fantastic. Girls in the audience, inside the small theater along Broadway from which Sullivan (and later, David Letterman and Stephen Colbert) broadcast his Sunday-night program, screamed so intensely and vocally that the mop-topped Fab Four could hardly be heard—even with microphones piped directly to the live feed.

Some seventy-three million people—equating to more than twenty-three million American homes, 45 percent of the entire U.S. population and 60 percent of all American televisions—sat transfixed in their living rooms and dens to see the Beatles' first live performance on U.S. soil. CBS received more than fifty thousand requests for tickets to the seven-hundred-seat theater.

Only seventy-seven days prior to the Beatles' appearance on *The Ed Sullivan Show*, President John F. Kennedy had been assassinated. By now, the country was ready for some much-needed joyful diversion, and it came in the form of four young lads from across the pond.

"Now yesterday and today, our theater's been jammed with newspapermen and hundreds of photographers from all over the nation, and these veterans agreed with me that this city never has witnessed the excitement stirred by these youngsters from Liverpool who call themselves the Beatles," said Sullivan in his introduction. "Now tonight, you're gonna twice be entertained by them. Right now, and again in the second half of our show. Ladies and gentlemen, the Beatles!"

And the British Invasion landed, in a splashy blast of driving drums, gritty guitars, cheerful harmonies, and lots and lots of hysterically screaming young ladies.

But, even while I was too young to remember this happening live, the thing that appeals to me about the Beatles' debut on American TV is that the nation felt this shared experience as one. We don't see that happening very much anymore, unless it's a national tragedy or emergency.

I can't remember the Beatles on *Ed Sullivan*, but I do remember watching that show every Sunday evening in later years. Laughing along with Stiller and Meara (yes, Ben Stiller's parents were tremendous comedians long before he got into the business), Burns and Schreibner, Allen and Rossi, and Topo Gigio the mouse. Sullivan would throw some crazy stunt acts such as acrobats, plate spinners, and magicians into the mix as fillers between the headliners, too. It made for a thoroughly enjoyable sixty minutes of entertainment with which to wind down a weekend.

No tricked-up competitions, no winners or losers, no drama or hyped conflict. Just a fun hour together at home with your family, and across the continent as the American family, sharing something on a regular basis.

Today, we have hundreds of channels on TV, plus video games, the Internet, texting, Tweeting, Skypeing, Hulu, Netflix, and whatever else from which to choose our entertainment. It's all so individualized now, which in some ways can be great. But in a larger sense, it takes away from the shared experience that used to be the norm.

Do I miss that? To borrow a phrase conveyed fifty-plus years ago by four young Liverpudlians—yeah, yeah, yeah.

Cub Scout Lamp

I t sat there, on the corner of the desk in my bedroom, from the time I was around nine until the day I left for college. Just a simple little lamp, nothing fancy. I didn't even turn it on all that much in those later years.

But I liked having it there, just to remind me.

We grew up in a neighborhood where the homes stood no more than ten feet apart. Where it took about fifteen paces to traverse the entire backyard. Where the steeply sloped alley behind the houses doubled as playground, basketball court, whiffle ball field, kick-the-can base, and daredevil bike rally track.

We all knew each other's business, which cut both ways, of course. On the downside, there couldn't be a lot of secrets when an open window—nobody had central air conditioning in our part of the world—served just as well as a wiretap planted in the kitchen next door.

But on the upside, we knew when a neighbor needed help or a hand—such as when the terrified screams that rent the air one early spring morning from the house across the street sent my mother running out our front door to find our neighbor hysterical beside her dead husband.

He had suffered a fatal heart attack while sitting in his favorite living room chair, waiting to drive her to work at the A&P. Within three minutes, though, most of the neighbor ladies had arrived, helping to calm and comfort our block's newest widow.

It was that kind of neighborhood. And now, nearly forty years after I left, the importance of it in shaping me and the other kids becomes more clear. One of the best examples remains that lamp on the corner of my bedroom desk.

My mom served as den mother to my Cub Scout troop, made up mostly of guys on our block and some other buddies from school. That meant the meetings took place in our basement, where we worked on projects and did activities to earn merit badges. I have no idea what badge this led to, but over the course of a series of Cub Scout meetings, we built our own lamps.

Mom pulled in reinforcements for this undertaking—namely Dad, whose skill at home repairs and building things still impresses and baffles all-thumbs me. He had the whole project mapped out: A bunch of preteen males would saw blocks of wood, drill holes into them, paint them with stain, assemble the wood pieces to make the base and stand, thread wire through a metal pole to deliver electricity, affix the bulb carriage, screw in the bulbs, and attach the lampshade.

He must have been either the most patient man on earth, the most confident, or the most off his rocker. But, doggone it, every one of us guys came out the other end of that odyssey with a perfectly functioning lamp. And, best of all, we had made it ourselves.

You hear about kids these days receiving trophies for participation. About parents hovering, interfering, refusing to let their kids learn by trial and error. In our crowded, tough-love city neighborhood, that sort of soft nonsense didn't happen.

Please don't misunderstand. We each got a trophy, all right. We built them in my cellar with our own hands at the tender age of nine. My Cub Scout lamp illuminated more than a desktop covered in homework and baseball cards and Hardy Boys books.

It illuminated the idea among my buddies and me that we could do anything, with hard work and the right guidance. Best of all, that light has yet to be extinguished, even if my Cub Scout lamp itself has long been lost. Thanks, Mom and Dad.

Diamond in the Dirt

The community park where the Little League baseball games got played as I grew up featured dirt. A lot of dirt. Dirt in the infield, dirt in the outfield, dirt in the dugouts. Dirt in your shoes, dirt in your eyes, dirt in your hair.

When you walked into your kitchen after an afternoon or early evening of hanging around that baseball field (and could it really be called a field, with such a dearth of grass?), your mother told you to march straight into the basement, get those clothes and shoes off, and head upstairs to take a shower. We didn't just clean this whole house to have you track clouds of dirt everywhere, like Pig-Pen in the Charlie Brown comics, you know.

But amid all that dirt came some of the happiest moments of childhood.

I might not know much, but I know myself, and I knew even then that when they passed out the athletic genes during DNA distribution, I must have been in the bathroom. As a result, I never tried out for Little League and never actually played a game on that field, other than when my friends would play pickup.

At the same time, I wanted to be around during the games, and not just a sorry baseball wanna-be observer on the rickety bleachers along the first-base line. So instead, I helped with everything else.

To be in the dugouts with my friends on the various teams, I learned to keep score in the official books for the league. As the half-inning ended and the players came from the field back into the dugout to bat, I loved crying out, "Johnson! Lewis! Trumble! And Ryan in the hole!" to let them know the batting order for the next inning. Little snatches of power. I didn't ask for much, really. Somewhere in the dusty, musty records of that borough where we lived, my scorebooks might lie in wait to this very day, aching, burning to be discovered and revealed to a waiting public. Or they got unceremoniously thrown into the garbage forty-plus years ago. Who knows?

Eventually, they let me chalk the lines on the field. The apex of nonplayer status. The zenith of responsibility for someone who would never be able to smack a ball over that plywood fence out there. It might have looked as if Otis the drunk from *The Andy Griffith Show* put the line down between third and home on occasion, but this was Little League for God's sake, not Yankee Stadium. Give me a break.

Then there was Mr. D., who umpired a lot of the games and who lived on my block. Mr. D. thought our little dirt field *was* Yankee Stadium, and he called balls and strikes with such aplomb and an over-the-top flourish that you couldn't help but enjoy. When Mr. D. umped a game, you were in for a show, baby.

Every time a pitcher threw one over the plate, or the batter swung and missed, the fireworks began. Mr. D., holding his chest protector in one hand and wearing his umpire's facemask, would quickly pivot to his right, point his finger with his free hand, and vigorously shake his arm and right leg in the air about ten times in unison, all the while shouting, "AIIIIIIEEEEEEEEEE!"

This happened with every strike. The whole game. It was an awesome display. One I'd never witnessed before or since. Unique in the annals of umpdom.

As the years passed, you started to worry that the man, with his high-volume, high-energy strike calls, might have a heart attack or something. Eventually he did, not on the field in his ump garb, but in his living room sitting in a recliner. It didn't seem fair somehow. Mr. D. deserved to go out with a bang, behind home plate, face down in that ubiquitous baseball dirt. Not enveloped in Naugahyde with his feet propped up and the TV blaring. He'd gotten cheated out of his big sendoff, the poor guy.

So as the major-league season continues, with its perfectly coiffed emerald sea in the outfield and the pristine uniforms, with a fresh, brand-new ball introduced every time another might have been slightly scuffed, I'll continue to think about that diamond in the dirt way back when, where we first learned to love the game.

In the Studio with Babe

J ust before Christmas, we went to a high school holiday concert, and watching the jazz ensemble play brought back wonderful memories of my days behind a drum set pounding out the beat with my high school friends on stage.

Most people don't know this, but I was quite the drummer as a kid and a teenager. It started when my folks wanted me to take piano lessons, actually. They drove me to a swanky part of town where this elderly gentleman taught young snots like me to play the piano.

Hated it immediately. HATE. ED. IT. Not the old dude so much, although he and his house did smell a little funky. A combination of cats, cigarettes, and Old Spice, if memory serves. Let it suffice to say that piano simply would never be my cup of tea, and leave it at that.

Then my dad suggested the drums. And the clouds parted, angels sang, a blinding light of happiness enveloped every cell in my seven-year-old corpus. I had come home to my calling. My true medium. My muse. Okay, I think you get the idea. Loved the drums. LOVE. ED. THEM.

Not sure how we found this tiny storefront studio, but every Saturday morning, either my mom or dad would drive me across town to take drum lessons from a cool, septuagenarian hipster who had gone by the name of Babe since the days when he played the drums touring with Bob Hope's band.

Babe never lost his skills with the sticks. He could play rings around the younger guys who worked for him in the shop. He hung out with Buddy Rich and Louie Bellson, two titans among drumming aficionados. Babe the Boss Man truly was boss, man. The best Saturday mornings were the ones when you had Babe teach your lesson, 'cause you hoped even a sliver of his cool and talent would rub off on you.

I studied at Babe's studio from second through eighth grade. My rubber-and-wood practice pad and thicker practice sticks (thicker so that when you mastered the sticking on a particular rhythmic pattern, it became even easier to play with standard thinner sticks), along with about eight years of lesson books, remain in a box in my storage shed even today. I flipped through a couple of them not long ago, and seeing "4-12-68" or "10-3-73" scribbled across the top of pages—marking the date of the next Saturday's lesson, by which time I needed to be able to play that set of pages—damn near blew my mind.

Those dates obviously passed a long, long, long time ago. But I can remember standing at the practice pad or sitting at the practice drum set in Babe's crowded little studio, with either him or one of the other instructors watching and listening, and feeling as if I always wanted to be there.

The skills learned in that studio led to some of my fondest pre-college memories. Playing with a community orchestra as the youngest member. Playing with a Revolutionary War re-enactment troupe during the American bicentennial in 1976. Playing in the marching band, jazz band, and concert band in high school. Even playing with a group, earning money on weekends at wedding receptions playing Top 40 songs, polkas, and such corny stuff as the "Alley Cat" dance. Beat the hell out of working at McDonald's, I'll tell you.

Not long ago, I drove through the neighborhood where Babe's studio had stood. It's in a part of town that has declined spectacularly since those happier days. But just cruising slowly by the old store-front—which must have changed hands plenty of times over the years—still made me smile. And made me want to pick up those sticks again more than ever.

Thanks, Babe. I know they're digging you laying down that solid beat today, somewhere above the clouds.

Narrowing the Gap

E ach of my kids had braces. Each of my kids needed to have his or her wisdom teeth pulled. Retainers, tightenings, chipmunk cheeks, twilight sedation, and some loopy re-entries when that happy juice started to wear off.

We did our part—more than our part if you ask me—helping one local oral surgeon's cash flow over the years with the wisdom teeth extractions. We got off a lot lighter with the braces, though. My cousin, the orthodontist, put us on the family plan, and I will be buying him drinks at any bar he chooses for the rest of our natural lives in gratitude.

But why did all three of my children require all this toothy attention when I never needed braces and never had one wisdom tooth even make an appearance? Not one. Ever.

In fact, my stupid mouth actually has two baby teeth that never left. To this day, there's a tooth on either side that I've had since toddlerdom. They moved in when the neighborhood was brand new, and there's been a lot of turnover. They've made friends with the bigger folks on each side of them. They haven't looked for something better after all this time, and it looks as though they have no intention of ever leaving. No adult teeth ever came in behind them, so they've been successful squatters for fifty-plus years.

I think, when my parts were being put together before being born, they ran out of teeth—a couple of grown-up samples and four wisdoms—at the DNA store. There are worse things.

Another anatomical anomaly: While growing up, my two front teeth had a gap between them so big, it looked like the Batcave. Adam West could have driven the Batmobile right through the front of my face.

Here's the difference between dental care in 1967 versus 2017, though. If I were a seven-year-old kid today, there'd be no question about getting braces. There'd be so much metal in my mouth, I'd look as if I belonged on an MTV rap video. I could pick up radio from Saskatoon. With every sneeze, garage doors in a two-mile radius would open inexplicably. Orthodontists in 2017 would be breaking down the door for a shot at my David Letterman-like dental Grand Canyon.

In time, my mom talked with our dentist—an older, no-nonsense gentleman named Dr. Ratchinski or something (this was a long time ago)—about narrowing the gap, as it were. This dentist had been around a long, long time and was not about to ship me off to some high-flyin' orthodontist.

"All of his other teeth are right where they should be," he declared. "It's just those two front ones. So here's what we're going to do."

He rummaged around in an adjacent room, came back, and placed a tiny object in my hand—no bigger than a dime, if that. A tiny rubber band, but one that had very little give to it. It took a lot to stretch it in other words.

"Now listen, Sonny. You put this around the outside of those two front teeth every day," he told me. "Push it up as high against your gums as you can. Nobody will be able to see it. You do this every day for a year, and your teeth will be perfect."

And you know something? It worked like a charm. It felt weird at first, but I learned how to move it up and down with my tongue, which gave me something to do when class got boring if nothing else.

The point is, there's no school like the old school. For the price (free!) of a handful of "gum bands," as we called them, this neighborhood dentist saved my folks thousands in bills for braces. He relied on tension and time instead of big-ticket tinsel.

How many other practices and products could be replaced with simpler, easier, less-expensive options? More than we realize is my bet. Thanks, Doc. Been smiling ever since.

Mike's Lunch

I t's astounding to think of how limited one's universe used to be while growing up.

For instance, a bunch of neighborhood kids and I walked to and from elementary school every day—including walking home for lunch and back to school, then walking home at the end of the day again. We had an established path of streets, staircases, and sidewalks, from which we never strayed. That wasn't because of any rules or safety concerns. It was simply because our familiar path represented the way to school and back home again. Period.

To have walked up the hill to school on the other side of the street? Unthinkable. Outrageous. Completely out of the question. The perception of our established universe precluded any such variations.

In the small business district of the neighborhood where we grew up, these guidelines also held. You bought your shoes at S&S Shoe Store. You got groceries at Kroger—maybe the A&P, in a pinch. You bought 45-rpm records for a dollar apiece at the Mount Oliver Record Shop. You killed time and maybe bought a model airplane kit at Bill & Walt's Hobby Shop.

And you ate hamburgers at Mike's Lunch. Hey, we didn't make the rules. That was just how things were in our preadolescent brains.

We never had the guts to actually speak to Mike, who we assumed was the angry guy with the apron frying up paper-thin patties, slapping them onto skimpy buns, and squirting brown mustard on them, whether you asked for brown mustard or not. We acquired a taste for those burgers, though. And it went way beyond any culinary qualifications.

Mike's Lunch meant so much more than hamburgers to us as kids. Mike's Lunch was where the cool kids went, not unlike Arnold's on the old *Happy Days* TV show. It looked like a beat-up old hole-in-the-wall, full of booths along one side and the grill, cash register, and bathrooms on the other. Yet, somehow, in the perspective of our limited universe, Mike's Lunch became almost intimidating.

It took some courage to place yourself into such an awesomely hip environment. Then to order a burger and actually eat it there? Lines got crossed. Reputations elevated. Swagger soared.

And the biggest proof of all that Mike's Lunch epitomized cool and dominance and superiority in our little early-'70s world? The Little League team it sponsored.

I was never much of an athlete, and my involvement in youth baseball revolved around keeping the written box scores in large score books for various teams. Our league sported four of them—Beckman Motors, Firemen, Kiwanis, and Mike's Lunch. Beckman Motors and Kiwanis most years fielded guys with similar talent levels. "Not great, but always giving a good effort" might be the kindest way of describing them. The Firemen squad played a little better.

But Mike's Lunch always kicked everybody else around. They were the New York Yankees of our little four-team league. I usually kept score for the other teams because I knew there wouldn't be much to mark down anytime those other poor chumps played Mike's Lunch—they were that good.

That was a long time ago, though, and one's universe changes and expands with the passing years. I took a drive recently along the path we walked to school as kids and couldn't believe how narrow the streets were and how short the walk seemed.

As I rode down the main drag of the old business district, I saw that all of those old stores have either converted to other establishments or been boarded up. Even the mighty Mike's Lunch. But back in the day, you sure couldn't get any cooler. Now, where's my brown mustard?

Miss Four of Diamonds

G rowing up in an urban middle-class neighborhood, boys like me dreamed of getting a minibike. And not a small bicycle, mind you, but a minibike—a miniature motorcycle.

The noise, the power, the ability to go a hell of a lot faster than your scrawny little knobbly kneed legs could take you. We knew of a couple of kids who actually got minibikes, and behind our Chamber of Commerce smiles, calculated to convey intense and sincere friendship—and nothing says friendship like letting a buddy take a spin on your minibike, right?—we secretly hated their guts. Mostly because they never—ever—let us ride.

So the best the rest of us adolescent yonkos could hope for came down to taping baseball cards to the rear posts of our regular bicycles so that when the back wheel started to rotate, the card would slap against the spokes and simulate the sound of a motorcycle.

Hey, when you're thirteen and broke, you make the most of the situation. We were MacGyvers before MacGyver was cool, all right?

Even this process required some forethought and careful evaluation. You didn't want to tape a Roberto Clemente card back there and let it take the tremendous beating those spokes were preparing to deliver. No, instead you fished out a handful of potential sacrificial lambs from your box of old baseball cards.

Guys like Vic Davalillo, yeah, he could get spoked. Milt May? Probably. You stopped and debated Steve Blass, though. He did win that seventh World Series game in Baltimore, but then the poor slob completely forgot how to pitch. Blass got the reprieve and was tossed back into the shoebox, but he'd be in the bullpen if the other two guys should flame out too fast.

While out pedaling around the neighborhood with two friends, our baseball cards emitting roars of simulated combustion-engine power, we took a break in a nearby park when my friend Mikey made one of the most interesting suggestions of my early teenagerhood.

He pulled out from his back pocket not a baseball card, but a playing card. And not just any playing card. This one had a naked girl on it.

Mikey had five older brothers, and he took full advantage of one of the great features of such a sibling setup: He had open access to all of their nasty, naughty, never-to-be-discussed-with-Mom-and-Dad items. As long as he didn't get caught, that is. Every couple of weeks, Mikey'd show up with bright red mark across his cheek, or a puffed-up eye. That's when we knew Mikey's big brothers had caught him messing with their stuff.

On this day, however, Mikey made it out of the house not only alive, but with one of the most hallowed treasures a gang of sheltered thirteen-year-olds could imagine: a card with the portrait of a girl with no clothes on.

"Okay, guys, who wants it for their bike?" Mikey asked.

"For our bikes?" cried Dean. "Mikey, are you nuts? We can't tape that to our bikes. Plus, why would you want to? We ought to find a good rock to hide that under so we can come out here all the time and look at it."

"Nah, I swiped this to go on somebody's bike," Mikey insisted. "It'll make the same sound, but whoever gets it will know how great his noisemaker really is! Let's shink on it. I got evens. Ready?"

After a couple of rounds of shink (where two guys put up fingers, with the winner determined by whether the total is an even or odd number), guess who got the naked-lady noisemaker?

So off came Vic Davalillo, and on went Miss Four of Diamonds. I wasn't sure it was better to go really fast, so that no one could see who was on that card, or to go really slow, so that no one cared. I'd never had a more self-conscious bike ride in my life.

That was, until we were pumping our bikes up the back alley, just as my mom started pulling her car into the garage as she came home from work.

"Hi, boys," she called to us, and I just kept pumping up the hill— no time to talk Mom, very busy here, need to keep moving, you know, pedal, pedal, pedal.

"Hey, come back here and say hi to your mom—what's the matter with you?" Mikey teased, a smirk beginning to form in the corner of his mouth, the bastard. He'd set me up.

"Look, we all put baseball cards on our spokes to make noise like a minibike," the shrimpy little sadist explained to my mother. "I have Johnny Bench on mine."

"Oh, that's nice," Mom replied. "Dean, who's on your—"

CRASH!

As I made a U-turn to come back to where they were talking, I, um, lost my balance and fell off the bike. An unbelievable coincidence, as it turns out.

"Are you all right? What happened?"

"I'm okay, Mom," I said with some difficulty. It was pretty hard to enunciate with all of that coated plastic on the roof of my mouth.

"Whose card is on your bike, honey?"

"Oh, my old one flew off. I'm putting Steve Blass on next."

Fifteen minutes later, we gathered in that park again. Miss Four of Diamonds, having been in my mouth all that time, lost some of her allure, to be sure. She never made it back onto any of our bikes again, but we did visit her regularly when we would pull her out from under a really good rock.

A MacGyver always makes do, you know.

Mrs. Gorinski

One otherwise nondescript Wednesday evening in 1973, Mrs. Gorinski rose from her Formica-top kitchen table, scraped her picked-over chicken bones into the garbage, and walked slowly over to the porcelain sink, wiping her hands on her apron. She leaned on the counter, looked out the window to the tiny backyard marked by burned-brown crabgrass, and started to cry.

Not heavy, heaving sobs, mind you. Just a welling up and a trickle down each cheek. The damp tracks that a woman of nearly sixty, widowed for some thirty years, her children all relocated to distant time zones, who rarely called or wrote and who held her grandchildren hostage from her, had earned.

Out that window she saw all the things she had planned to do, to make of her life, alongside her beloved husband. They had met near a waterfall during the Great Depression, she loved to tell people. Her family had pulled together enough bits of food for a modest outdoor picnic, and he had a job as a surveyor with the Works Progress Administration, clearing land for a state park.

Even from a hundred feet away, as she would recount the story, their eyes locked and their futures fused. It took him two months to track her down, asking anybody who visited that waterfall if they knew the girl in the dark blue dress with the rose print.

They married within a year and got straight to business, producing three children, a boy and two younger sisters. When the war came, he got drafted and assigned to the Army Corps of Engineers for the European Theater. While surveying a ravine where a bridge needed to be built, a mortar shell exploded nearby, leaving his remains never to be recovered. He was, literally, gone.

Left to fend for herself at twenty-eight, with three small children in tow, the temptation to give up, to abandon those kids to the mercies of foster homes, to simply lose her mind and run screaming into the night—she felt them all but succumbed to none. She, like so many people on the front lines overseas and on the home front back here, simply did what had to be done. The Greatest Generation, indeed.

She took in sewing and cleaning work to earn money. She took care of those young ones with all of the heart and muscle and courage she could muster. She held her family together and taught them how to create a life of value by showing them. A lesson she believed they learned, although her deep, crushing loneliness would prove otherwise at times.

During those long, trying years, however, she did surrender one thing to her grief. She never wore that dark blue dress with the rose print again.

All of these images swirled around her mind as she gazed out her back window when a ringing phone startled her back into conscious reality. Reaching across the kitchen to the wall-mounted rotary set, she answered and began speaking to one of her neighbors down the street. Seems this nice young wife and her husband would be going out to a dinner on Saturday night and wanted to know if Mrs. Gorinski was available to babysit.

"Oh, I don't know. … Your children don't even really know me, do they? … It's been quite awhile since I took care of such young kids. … Well, that's awfully nice of you to say, but I'm not sure I'm who you really need for this. … Yes, well, thank you for asking anyway."

The next afternoon, Mrs. Gorinski could be found in her little backyard, pinning up laundry onto a clothesline to dry, as the young wife from down the street walked by on her way back from the neighborhood store.

"Have you found anyone to watch your kids yet? ... Oh, I'm sorry. ... How many kids do you have again? ... A boy and two younger girls? ... Is that right? ... You know, if the offer still stands, I think I could do it after all."

With forty-eight hours to prepare, she went to work, just like in the old days. The needle and thread might not have moved with quite the speed as in her prime, but she got the job done.

And when Mrs. Gorinski knocked on her neighbors' door that Saturday evening, to take care of that boy and his two younger sisters, even as a tiny tear of joy trickled down her cheek, she looked wonderful in a slightly let-out dark blue dress with the rose print.

Walls

Negotiations had hit a snag. The two sides needed to walk away from the bargaining table for a while. Good thing, because their respective mothers had begun calling them to dinner anyway.

I had three shoeboxes full of baseball cards, purchased at the local family-owned corner store, quickly looked at and then unceremoniously tossed into those boxes over the years. Now, this being the summer between grade school and high school, those cards seemed like kid stuff.

I'd pulled out all the good Pirates players and kept them for myself. I wasn't a complete idiot. But the rest of them? Who cares?

Who cares? Stanny, the goofy kid five doors down, that's who. Two or three years younger than me, Stanny loved all things baseball. ERAs, batting averages, career strikeouts, on-base percentages—he knew them all. When I bought a pack of baseball cards, if there weren't any Pirates in there, then the stick of bubble gum became priority one. Not Stanny. He was one of those kids who looked at the back of the card with all of the statistics first, not the picture on the front. The pasty little weirdo.

And he wanted those three shoeboxes of mine something fierce. Hence, the high-stakes negotiations.

He made some halfhearted offers. Stickers, photos, refillable pencils, all sorts of crap he didn't want—and so he thought I would want it? Things got heated, and then we had to break for supper. When bargaining started up again that evening, I finally said, "Stanny, you need to give me something I want as much as you want these baseball cards. That's how this works. Quit goofing around. Do you have anything like that or not?"

Dejected, rejected, resigned to failure, he halfheartedly walked out of his living room, went upstairs, and came back down with something folded under his arm. "I don't think you'll like this, but it's the only thing I could think of," Stanny said with his hangdog expression. "My brother got it at a concert or something."

He handed it to me, a red-and-blue cloth of some sort. Fully unfurled, I saw it in all its glory. Not an American flag, but a banner with the logo of the band Chicago on it. My favorite band of all time! I shoved my baseball cards at Stanny, and without saying "thank you" or "good-bye" or "take a hike," I ran out his front door and up the street to my house, where I found a hammer and some nails and immediately tacked that Chicago flag into the wood paneling on the wall above my bed.

Mom and Dad weren't all that thrilled with the redecorating job, especially the nail-pounding part, but that banner stayed there all through my high school years, as did two other notable mementos.

One featured a poster of the Dallas Cowboys Cheerleaders. This might sound strange to anyone who knows me well as a lifelong diehard bleeding-black-and-gold fan of the Pittsburgh Steelers, since my team met—and defeated—the Cowboys in two classic Super Bowls of the 1970s. How, then, could I possibly commit such heresy as to have a 24-by-36-inch poster of their cheer squad on my bedroom wall?

Because I was a fourteen-year-old hormonal American male with no real-life prospects. Duh. I think, by today's standards, the sexy quotient of my cheerleaders poster would rate no more than a three, maybe a four. But back then? Wow. Wow. Wowee wow-wow.

The other wall-mounted treasure came as the result of hero worship. I'd gone with a friend and fellow high school band drummer to see a Buddy Rich concert one evening. Buddy played those drums like no one I had ever seen. His sticking so unbelievably fast, his meter perfect, his ability to drive the rest of his jazz band through number after number simply amazing. He gave my friend and me something to shoot for as jazz drummers. We never quite made it, to no one's surprise, but we sure had something to shoot for.

We hung around after the show, walked up to the foot of the stage, and hoped to say hello and shake Buddy's hand. But we ended up with more than that. He not only talked with us, but he gave my friend the drumsticks he had used that night, and he gave me his sweaty towel—complete with his autograph!

I suspect Mom wanted to tear that thing off my wall a thousand times and toss it into the washer, but she never did. It remained there through high school, too.

The night I ran out of Stanny's house was the last time I ever saw him. My Chicago flag, my Cowboys Cheerleaders poster, and my autographed Buddy Rich towel all have disappeared into memory, as well.

But I bet Stanny held onto those baseball cards for the next forty years and has probably cashed them in for millions. The little creep. I never was that sharp a negotiator.

Queenie, My First Friend

My first friend lived next door, in a neighborhood where you had no choice but to be close to your neighbors. The houses couldn't have been more than ten feet apart, so when you wanted to spend time in your backyard, it became a public event. The family who lived one door down from us on our slanted street had kids older than me, except for their youngest.

Being the same age as me, my first friend and I spent time together as preschoolers, then as kindergarten kids, and finally as first-graders, walking to school together with the older siblings from next door.

To the mother, my first friend was the apple of her eye. To the older brothers, well, they sure noticed that—which is how they came up with the name they used to tease my first friend.

They called her Queenie because she was the only female child in the bunch, plus the baby of the family, which meant she held a unique place in her mother's heart. Yeah, my very first friend was the girl next door.

Queenie held her own, living in a house with older brothers. A tomboy, she liked to run and play kick the can in the front street with the rest of the kids on our block. She had a beautiful collie as a pet and would get that dog to leap up and put its two front paws on her shoulders from behind so that they could walk around the yard together. I always thought that was the funniest thing going.

As we advanced through elementary school, we each made new friends and ran with different kids, but I always felt a special kinship with Queenie. We saw each other through the cyclone fence separating our backyards every day. We grew up together. We knew each other from our earliest recollections. She felt like another sister to me.

I can recall hearing the news the morning of New Year's Day 1973 that Pirates superstar Roberto Clemente had died the night before in a plane crash while on a humanitarian mission. Hours earlier, at midnight, Queenie and her family had been on our front porch making noise and ringing in the new year together. With news of Clemente's death, we could only look through that fence at each other and feel as if a shared hero had been cruelly torn from us.

Occasionally we'd bump into each other walking home from high school. On one of those walks, she pleaded with me to teach her the words to the alma mater, and of course I did. Even all those years after walking to first grade together, I still wanted to help her out when I could. She was my friend, after all.

Over time she would bear the loss of her father and brothers, leaving just her and her mother. When I could attend those sad services, I did. When I couldn't, because of distance or time, I hope she knew my prayers tried to close the gap.

There's something about your first friend that engraves something on your heart that's tough to match. I never once called her Queenie. I had no reason to use that title with her.

Even though our lives have diverged and I haven't seen her in a long, long time, she was, is, and will always be, my first friend—running around the front street with our gang, parading around her yard with a collie up on its hind legs trotting behind her, singing our alma mater while strolling down the sidewalk, sharing a childhood and adolescent friendship through the back fence, being like another sister—and that's title enough.

Mick and Fee

I n the back room, just steps from the crowded shelves, lunch meat cooler, candy counter, and pinball machine of their busy neighborhood store, hung an old photograph in a weathered frame.

In it, a black-and-white image shows Michelangelo Rosetti and Fiona Coralini standing, looking straight into the camera, young and scared and ready to step into the future as a married couple. The photograph, taken nearly fifty-three years earlier in 1931 inside a hillside chapel rising above the Adriatic Sea, offered the sole remaining tie to the old country for Mick and Fee. When they came through Ellis Island as newlyweds, their minds and hearts became American.

With a cousin serving as their sponsor, Mick worked odd jobs in construction while Fee jarred pickles in a factory until they had saved enough to purchase a house on a busy corner of a tightly packed city neighborhood. Before long the first floor transformed into a store, stocked with just enough inventory of household staples, milk, snacks, tobacco, pop, and candy to become an indispensable hub—the center of commerce and conversation for decades.

A beat-up cash register stood on the counter, but pretty much in name only. Mick did his addition on the backs of cardboard boxes and empty cigarette cartons, making change in a cash drawer that never quite closed all the way. They knew everybody who came into their place, so who needs receipts or inventory records?

When the Pepsi guy came, the Pepsi guy got paid and stocked the shelf with some bottles. When April 15 rolled around, they gave the IRS their best guess. If you were a little short on buying a half-pound of chipped ham today, you could get Mick next time. You gotta feed those kids, right? What's the big deal? We're all friends here.

Mick and Fee opened their doors when the sun rose and closed after Huntley-Brinkley finished the news on TV with that intense music from Beethoven's Ninth. They never conducted business on Sunday and closed up shop from noon to 3 p.m. every Good Friday. Good Catholics—although, strangely, no one ever seemed to spot them in church.

One curious thing about Mick and Fee remained, however. For a few years, they'd close the store every Tuesday afternoon around four but never said why. The neighborhood regulars would ask but never got anything more specific than, "Oh, we had to." Or, "Heck, you know." Or, "Ah, nothing important."

They had reached well into their seventies by this point, hair a little thin on top and waists a little thick around the middle, and the first wave of local scuttlebutt guessed that one of them had taken ill and needed some kind of treatment. Their continued presence in the store, hale and hearty and as full of piss and vinegar as ever, seemed to quell that rumor. What Tuesday-evening secret caused these two septuagenarians to disappear week after week?

The answer could be found in that old photograph on the wall. Mick came to America determined to make a successful life for Fee and their eventual family (they produced five daughters before all had been said and done). He worked with his back and arms and hands at first and then became a small retail merchant. He provided his girls a life of modest means, a safe home, food on the table, a father's protection and support.

Yet a fire glowed deep in the eyes of that fresh, young, terrified groom inside that picture frame. You had to look so closely, so deeply, to spot it, but it absolutely burned. One evening, after locking the front door, turning out the lights at the store, and walking past the photo on the way upstairs to their living quarters, Mick froze.

Something about that photo, that look in his eyes. He'd shuffled past it thousands of times and never gave it a second thought. But this night, it rocked him like a sucker punch to the gut. A round-house smack that took his breath away—all in all, a fairly alarming proposition for an old seventy-something coot like him.

Reaching the top of the steps, he saw Fee in front of the stove warming some soup for dinner. He all but ran over to her, wrapped his leathery old arms around her from behind, and declared his epiphany. And every Tuesday night from then on, he and she would close early and go someplace special.

Occasionally, a mother would send one of her kids up to Mick and Fee's for some milk or a loaf of Town Talk bread on a late Tuesday afternoon, forgetting—until the little missionary came home empty-handed. What is going on up there with those two? Where do they go? And why won't they tell us?

But while that milk-and-bread-less mother contemplated those questions, in the activity room of a small municipal building across town, Fee sat off to the side, quietly reading a library book, while her husband—the fiery-eyed man from the Adriatic—stood amid a circle of people. A circle of friends. Of simpaticos.

And read from his tattered handwritten notebook of original poetry.

Boy, if the Pepsi guy could see him now.

Talent Show

Every year, like clockwork, the three brothers got the nod. Grandma's basement, in front of the washtubs. Showtime. Down the stairs they came, three cousins of mine, bathrobes cinched tight, aluminum foil crowns perched atop their close-shaven heads, each carrying a decorated shoebox—gold, frankincense, and myrrh—and singing "We Three Kings" to the rest of our extended family, sitting piled onto good Catholic wooden church folding chairs. The annual Christmas Grandchildren Talent Show had begun.

I typically had to drag out a drum and do a few basic flourishes with my sticks. Another cousin performed a jazz dance routine. Others told stories or jokes, or showed us a particularly impressive school art project, or recited a poem that had been memorized, or sang other Christmas carols.

To a non-family observer, the whole thing probably would have reeked of a bunch of marginally talented city kids being coerced into doing their limited repertoire in front of parents, aunts, uncles, and grandparents—with the irresistible lure of heaping mounds of home-made spaghetti and juicy, sauce-laden meatballs to follow as a reward. Middle-class Italian heritage bribery at its finest.

But to the adults crammed into that little basement theater, the ones whose kids got trotted in front for their five minutes of family fame, this is what made the holiday so special. So unforgettable. So ingrained into the fabric and DNA of our clan. They loved every young performer, because they loved every one of us kids.

One year some cousins brought cousins from the other side of their family to Grandma's. When the Three Kings kicked off the extravaganza, these other kids didn't know what hit them. Act after act, like a pint-sized *Ed Sullivan Show* knockoff, they'd never seen anything like it, you could tell. When it was all over, and all the applause and hugs had been distributed, they looked shell-shocked. We had rocked their little Christmas world.

They never came around to Grandma's on Christmas Day again, though, now that I think of it. Rookies.

In time, naturally, my cousins grew up, got married, started their own families, just as I did. When my kids were little, we had them join their cousins at their grandma's house each Christmas, just as we did. And you bet they put on a talent show, just as we did. You can't fight genetics, I guess.

But that kind of family-only tradition is what makes Christmas unlike any other day of the year, don't you think? Sure, there's the excitement, anticipation, and magic of Christmas Eve. Then the mad rush and euphoria of Christmas morning, opening presents and enjoying your new toys. But when all of that's over and it's time to gather together—just because you want to be together—and enjoy each other's company, get a kick out of a little kid's jokes, and realize how very, very blessed you truly are? That's when it all gets real. As real as it can get.

My favorite part of the holiday movie *A Christmas Story* isn't when Ralphie gets his Red Ryder rifle or when his friend gets his tongue frozen to the flagpole. It's near the end of the film when his mom and dad sit quietly on Christmas night watching the snowfall outside the window. Showered in love and contentment. Peace on Earth, indeed.

I'd love to get my three cousins together again right now and re-create their classic "We Three Kings" routine, just for old time's sake. You bring the bathrobes and shoeboxes, fellows, I'll bring the aluminum foil, and we'll get together downstairs in front of the washtubs one last time. What do you say?

Merry Christmas, everyone.

Replacing Clark

"Hey Pal, hey Skip, hey Chief, hey Buddy, hey Buster, hey Friend, hey Champ, hey—"

Clark the Barber would rattle off these calls to the next kid in line at his hole-in-the-wall shop, around the corner from our neighborhood strip mall, until you clambered up onto his worn-leather chair.

Clark's Barbershop became one of those places that got fixed in your memory, because nothing ever changed there, starting with Clark himself. Standing close to six feet tall with a sandy, reddish crop of hair himself, Clark wore a white barber's smock and always seemed to be snapping a pair of scissors in his hand, whether he was in the process of cutting someone's hair or not. That jar of mysterious blue liquid that allegedly kept combs and stuff sanitized always sat there on the shelf below the mirror.

He held court behind a green faux-leather barber's chair, with a web of small creases and cracks on the seat, the little silver ashtray flaps on the arms, and the chunka-chunka hydraulics set to work as Clark foot-pumped the chair higher. A big plate-glass window with Clark's name painted backward provided the portal through which you could look out and see your buddies making faces at you while Clark clipped away at your mop-top.

And then there stood the two crowning jewels of Clark's small kingdom: the greatest collection of *Archie* comic books in town and the Pepsi cooler where you could help yourself to a miniature bottle of pop while waiting your turn and enjoying the latest adventures of Betty, Veronica, Jughead, and the rest of the Riverdale High gang.

I loved going to Clark's for haircuts and did so until I started high school, when everything changed. No, not with me, but with Clark.

He'd been on his feet, snipping away, for a very long time, and I guess he either got tired or decided he'd made enough money by that point. Or maybe he lost his shirt giving away all that Pepsi. Whatever the reason, Clark hung up his shears and retired.

After years of comfort, familiarity, and free comic books, suddenly it came time to find another barber. The only trouble was, in the mid-1970s, barbers had become quite hard to come by. All I had to pick from were so-called stylists.

Being the frugal, pragmatic type—also known as a broke high school kid without a car—I started going to the stylist within the shortest walking distance from my house, a fellow who went by the last name of Barbieri, which to this day I believe was a crass marketing ploy to make rubes like me think they were getting some Italian-trained hotshot hacking away at their heads.

My new stylist started by dunking me into a sink for a shampoo and then used a razor to "shape" and "contour" and "stagger" my manly locks into something unique and stunning. He wrapped things up by slapping a lot of "product" all over my scalp and using a hair dryer to bring the dynamic episode to a breathtaking, flourishing finish.

All I could think of was, "Toto, I don't believe we're at Clark's anymore." The bill—which included purchases of some hoity-toity special shampoo and conditioner, along with styling mousse or some such crap—sure didn't resemble Clark's, either. With Clark, you sat down, he cut your dry old hair, he brushed you off, kicked you out of the chair, collected his dough, and started his call for the next guy in line.

Thus began a lifetime of searching for a person to cut my hair who I really like. Some of these relationships have lasted longer than others, but none has ever really taken root, so to speak. All I want is a comfortable, safe, reliable haircut. And maybe a couple of comic books and a free Pepsi. I put it to you, is that really too much to ask?

Hey Pal, hey Skip, hey Chief, hey Buddy, hey Buster, hey Friend, hey Champ. I'm still here. Still waiting.

The Mystery of Buck

As one plows one's way through the different phases of life, certain people take center stage and remain there. Others capture the spotlight for a time then fade away. Then there are the scores of peripheral players who come and go, some making a more memorable—although fleeting—mark than others.

One such person in my life was Buck Nelson.*

Buck seemed to live at the municipal park near the house where I grew up. An older gentleman—although I'm probably past the age now that he was then—Buck stood as the authority on all things sports that happened at that park. He coached the best of four Little League baseball teams each year, he also held the whistle for the Pee-Wee football team that represented our little borough, and everyone simply deferred to Buck on any decision or question regarding equipment, the use of fields for practice, anything.

Buck ran our town's sports activities for young kids. Period.

Now, faithful readers of mine can tell you that the sum total of my athletic prowess wouldn't fill half a thimble. But that didn't mean I never hung around that park. Pickup games happened all the time on those fields, and I'd bang around with my buddies, having fun,

---

* This is a fictitious name.

knowing that no one kept score in a book and no spectators sat in the stands.

When the game didn't count, that's when I felt comfortable playing. When it did, that's when I felt comfortable watching or helping out. A simple rule that seemed to work pretty well.

So, in my usual role of observer and hanging-around guy, the continuous presence of Buck—even then, from an elementary-school kid's perspective—always struck me as a little odd. Looking back now, many decades later, that sense of unease has only grown.

None of my friends ever told me about anything weird or strange or questionable going on regarding Buck, and I certainly never got close to that inner circle of juvenile jockdom where Buck took the lead. Chances are that nothing weird or strange or questionable ever happened to anybody, and I'm sure Buck's gone on to his eternal reward—or punishment—by this time, anyway.

But isn't it disquieting that such thoughts and suspicions have become almost the assumed truth these days? That the news, nearly every day, features at least one story of a parent, or parent's boyfriend, or teacher, or coach, or priest, or scoutmaster doing something so heinous and reprehensible to a child?

No doubt, the vast—vast—majority of adults who take on leadership roles involving children do so with a clean heart and a sense of honor and duty. And they should be thanked and respected, even as safeguards should remain in place and accountability must be insisted upon at all times.

There's nothing in the world more valuable and precious than a child's innocence. Once it has been damaged or shattered, it can never be restored. Anyone who does so deserves equally dreadful recompense.

So, did Buck Nelson behave responsibly all those years, with all those young boys, in that municipal park decades ago? Only he and his youthful charges will ever know. I certainly hope so and have no evidence after all this time to seriously think otherwise. But the fact that it still raises doubts in my mind might be the more troubling truth of all.

The Two-Pole Tower

I n the park where my friends and I spent most of our free time as kids stood a tower comprising two thick, enormously tall, wooden telephone poles.

Some sort of contraption rested at the top of this tower, connected to the two poles, but we could never figure out what it was, what it did, or why it stood looming over the swing sets, seesaws, sliding boards, and sandboxes we so often frequented.

Even more, we didn't much care. The two-pole tower simply existed. It was just there, so while it might have been a bit of a mystery to a bunch of grade-school kids, it never made much of a difference to us.

The two-pole tower did work great as home base for games of tag or release or hide-and-seek. It made an easy place to agree to meet after school as the starting point of our afternoon adventures. The two-pole tower might have been somewhat of an anomaly, not really blending in with the rides and ball fields of our neighborhood park, but so what? It meant nothing. Just a two-pole tower somebody stuck there long before any of us showed up.

It wasn't until many years later that I learned the true purpose of the two-pole tower—and it scared the living tarp out of me.

The tower stood higher than anything else in that park, for a good reason. The poles were larger, thicker, and sturdier than standard utility poles, also for a good reason. The contraption at the top never made sense to us as kids, because it had never been used in our lifetimes, and again, for a good reason.

And what was that good reason, you ask? Our mysterious two-pole tower actually had been used during World War II as a blackout warning siren for our sleepy little neighborhood. When the siren at the peak of the tower sounded, during nighttime drills, people had to turn off all of their indoor and outdoor lights, draw all of their shades (which had been painted black on the side facing outward), and turn off their car headlights.

Why? To practice self-preservation. To not give enemy warplanes any visible targets to drop bombs on. To keep them and their children alive.

Can you imagine having to take these measures against the potential threat of airborne bombers cruising over your comfortable suburban cul-de-sac? That remains a reality in too many parts of the world, even today. But thinking of it happening—or even practicing over the chance of it happening—in the community where I grew up is simply mind-blowing.

The art of war has changed since the 1940s, of course. Today we have unmanned drones, GPS satellite targeting, and all forms of long-distance destruction available. It keeps the side that's doing the shooting safer, the more miles it can keep away and apart from where the bombs are landing, I suppose. Still makes it difficult for me to accept the rationale behind war in the first place.

Wouldn't it be great if, like that neighborhood park my friends and I enjoyed all those years ago, we needed only the swing sets, seesaws, sliding boards, and sandboxes? If people could just live alongside each other in peace and joy and friendship?

It's too bad that idyllic dream has to acknowledge the potential terror signified by that two-pole tower. It's too damn bad.

Rocco, My True-Life Hero

E very summer, it seems, we get inundated with movies about superheroes. Men and women who do amazing things against tremendous odds while always keeping their humanity and their compassion for other people front and center.

But I knew a real-life hero when I was small. I knew him for only a short time, and the memories for me get a little fuzzy around the edges. His story, as recalled and retold by my predecessors, though, fills in the blanks and creates a tale of courage and caring and inspiration—enough to rival, and even surpass, any filmed fiction currently playing in your local Cineplex.

This hero's name was Rocco, and he was my grandfather.

Rocco came into the world just prior to the turn of the twentieth century, born in Abruzzi, a fishing and farming village on the Adriatic Sea in southern Italy. His formal education ended in the fourth grade when he began working to help support his family's olive oil-processing enterprise.

While he had a loving family and lived in beautiful surroundings (Abruzzi today has become a high-end luxury resort destination for wealthy Europeans), Rocco dreamed of life in America. And at the tender age of fifteen, he boarded a boat—alone—for the long journey, armed only with a shovel and the equivalent of fifteen American dollars.

Onboard the ship—where he rode on the crowded, windowless bottom deck—Rocco by chance discovered a distant cousin, thus making the trek much less lonesome. Once the two cousins came through Ellis Island, however, they contracted typhoid fever, and Rocco's newfound friend died. Alone, unable to speak English, Rocco arranged to bring his cousin's body and have it buried in Pittsburgh, where Rocco's sponsor lived and was waiting for him. Our family still visits that lonely gravestone today.

Rocco and his sponsor began a contracting business, which grew and did well, even surviving the Great Depression. He was so skilled at his craft that he once won a contest for bricklaying to build a new street. During World War II, black marketeers approached Rocco to siphon gasoline, which was strictly rationed, from his company's onsite gas pump. He immediately threw them off his property, insulted that anyone would even consider such a dishonest thing during a time of national emergency. His code of honor, honesty, and humility remained untarnished his entire life.

As the war raged in Europe, Rocco's family had to flee into the hills to seek safety from the Nazis, who had overrun their village and sacked their home. When the war ended, Rocco returned to help them rebuild, contributing his contractor's talents, along with money and most of his own clothing he had packed for the trip. For the remainder of his days, he continued to send funds and supplies to his people living along the Adriatic.

His five children grew to be successes in their personal and professional lives. And of his nineteen grandchildren, there's not a bad apple in the bunch. Doctors, lawyers, builders, medical researchers, artists, entrepreneurs—even a professional writer. If there's any better or stronger or more gratifying legacy, I'd love to hear it.

Rocco passed from this earth in 1969, at the age of seventy-three, after a series of medical issues. As the paramedics carried him out of the home he had built with his bare hands, the home where he had run his business, raised his family, and enjoyed his grandchildren so much, his doctor was heard to say, "Good-bye, you dear man."

I wasn't quite nine years old when he died, so my memories center more around sitting under the backyard grape arbor with my grandpap, munching on the juicy grapes, and sharing the chunks of mozzarella and pepperoni that he loved to slice and snack on. Or taking rides in his car to run errands, or visiting a piece of farmland he owned far from the city. Little moments that meant so much, thinking back now.

As a little boy, I thought of Rocco as a hero because he was such a big presence with such a gentle soul. As a man, knowing and appreciating all that he accomplished, I think of him as hero for pretty much the same reasons.

He did amazing things against tremendous odds while always keeping his humanity and his compassion for other people front and center. What's more, unlike the costumed characters on a movie screen, Rocco's story is true.

That's inspirational. That's an enormous legacy to live up to. And most of all, that's downright heroic.

The Visible Man

Growing up in a small borough, with its own park, its own theater, its own library, and its own three-block "downtown" business district, we had it made. My friends and I could walk everywhere, see or do or buy anything we wanted, and never break a sweat making it home for dinner on time.

A couple of the favorite haunts during any stroll through the neighborhood shops included the record store—where you could peruse the racks of 45s (we didn't have the dough for a full-blown album) until the little guy who owned the place started to get sore at us for not actually buying anything—and the hobby shop, where all of the coolest airplane and sports-car plastic model sets sat on shelves, just waiting for young bucks like us to take them home.

During one such venture into the hobby shop, for some reason I split off from the fifth-grade formation—went rogue, I suppose—and headed over to a different display of model kits, where one caught my eye and tenaciously held on like an angry pit bull.

The Visible Man.

The model displayed just what it sounded like: a clear plastic encasement in the shape and form of a grown human male, with every organ, nerve, vein, artery, and bone placed perfectly inside. My imagination fired, creativity inspired, I asked the owner of the store what The Visible Man cost. When they revived me off the floor, I left, dejected, and walked home.

Promoting the high-quality educational value of this model kit to my parents, we arrived at a deal whereby I cut the grass and did some other jobs around the house in exchange for funds sufficient to purchase The Visible Man. And before you knew it, there he was, on the desk in my room. Inscrutable, immovable, impeccable. Just waiting to be assembled into pristine formation.

I mean, how hard could it be? The directions looked pretty clear. And, honestly, how many bones and organs and stuff could actually be in a man's anatomy? I mean, come on! This was a one-afternoon job for a ten-year-old kid with good grades, tops.

Three weeks later, I'm sitting there with a plastic man who looked as if he just got extracted from a twelve-car pileup with the Jaws of Life. I couldn't fit one more thing into this guy's abdomen, yet I sat there enraged, holding a spleen or a pancreas or a liver or some damn thing. How could there be all these leftover parts? (Little did I know this adventure would serve as a precursor to scores of bookshelf, dresser, and other demented IKEA projects in later life.)

Eventually I figured the hell with it; my Visible Man would just have to go through life without a liver, or whatever that thing was, and hope for a transplant later.

Then it came time to paint in the veins and arteries. And the wheels really came off. One slip of the paint brush, maybe. You wipe it off and try again. But after about eighteen mistakes—while continuously getting the red veins mixed up with the blue arteries—that little plastic bastard came *this* close to going in the garbage.

Soon, my Visible Man became invisible, going back into his box and down into the cellar, where bad toys go to die. Seven years later, I left for college and never gave him a second thought. He's undoubtedly in some landfill today, still waiting for that liver transplant.

Come to think of it, I probably should have gotten The Visible Woman instead. Even if her innards never got assembled properly, at least the outer shell could have kept a fifth-grade boy busy.

The Yogi Splinter

Why do some apparently insignificant events from decades past stick to the brain like Velcro? The human mind must be wired to insist on closure, a sense that a matter has been settled to one's satisfaction, before that nagging memory can be released at long last.

Or, in my case, maybe I'm just a nut who can't let some things go. You make the call.

Six or seven years old, a little kid in a middle-class neighborhood in the city, and I wanted what a lot of other boys in that situation wanted. A dog. A pet. A buddy to play and mess around and get into trouble with.

And, like most young boys, I found ways to insufferably make this particular argument over and over with my parents, until finally they relented and we went to the local animal shelter to do a little window-shopping. Yeah, window-shopping my foot. I knew we were coming home with a dog that day, and so we did.

Looking at all the puppies available, my eye landed on a white-and-brown speckled beagle, and it was game over. My dad took care of whatever paperwork and payment they required, and we left for home with my new doggie. I named him Yogi, probably after Yogi Bear, which had been a popular cartoon at the time.

We fixed a little doghouse for Yogi on the back porch, because one of the ground rules was that he would not have free run of the inside of the people house. I took care of his food and water—or, I did so as well as any little kid can—and made sure he got his exercise.

Being a pup, Yogi did his share of chewing up carpet and drapes, which never earned him high scores with my folks. But more important, being a beagle, Yogi barked. A lot. And had the smell of a hound dog, which can be rather distinctive. The houses in our neighborhood had been built very close to each other, so the joys and the issues of keeping a beagle puppy—who slept outdoors, no less—became a community proposition.

Yogi did his best to be a good dog, and I did my best to be a good dog owner. But sometimes what sounds like a great idea in concept loses its luster in practical application. But even I wasn't ready for what happened next.

One summer morning, after we'd had Yogi for about a month, I went downstairs to check on him and give him fresh food and water. I looked on the back porch in his little shelter. No Yogi. I looked all over our tiny backyard. Not there, either. In the garage? Nope. The neighbors' yards? Up and down the front street and back alley? Not a trace. Yogi was gone.

I was told he must have run away, wriggled under the gate in the back fence somehow and took off. And I guess that made some sense. Yet he'd never tried to run off before, I couldn't help thinking to myself. It felt devastating, sure, knowing that my dog was gone. But a little splinter of doubt about what really happened also began to gnaw and knead itself into my subconscious—a situation that would continue unabated for some forty-five years, until just a few days ago.

During a recent get-together at my present home, I was talking with my dad when my yellow lab came up to us. That got us talking about my very first dog all those years ago in the old house when he said, "Yeah, we had to take him back to the shelter."

"I *knew it*!" I exclaimed. "I knew Yogi didn't run away!"

"No, he didn't. But that was the explanation that we thought you could accept. We weren't ready for a dog back then."

Perspectives change, of course. After my wife and I have now raised three grown children, I appreciate what happened to Yogi as responsible parenting and gracious neighboring. No hard feelings. I hope Yogi eventually found a little kid and a family better equipped to give him an awesome life, barky and smelly as it might have been.

But best of all, it feels great to finally remove that nagging, jagging, pestering, festering splinter from my psyche. Closure is a wonderful thing.

Mrs. Mills, Capitalist

The magical pennant run now being waged by my beloved Pittsburgh Pirates, twenty years in coming, got me thinking about something that happened more than forty years ago, when the Bucs won it all in 1971.

Ten years old and a dyed-in-the-wool Pirates fan, I knew they were gonna go all the way that year. So did all of my buddies in my neighborhood. We followed the standings in the paper every day, we knew the "magic number" needed to clinch the division title. It was a great summer to be a city punk in Pittsburgh.

Since we wore our love for Roberto Clemente, Willie Stargell, Steve Blass, Manny Sanguillen, Richie Hebner, Bill Mazeroski, Al Oliver, Bob Robertson, and all of the Buccos—even Manager Danny Murtaugh—emotionally on our sleeves anyway, we all had the great idea to do it literally, too.

We hopped a streetcar to the Honus Wagner Sporting Goods store Downtown and each plunked down $3.50 for a round, black-and-gold cloth patch with the Pirates logo on it—the one from the Three Rivers Stadium era, the guy wearing the big pirate hat with the skull and crossbones on it. Mrs. Mills, the mom of one of the guys in our gang who lived across the back alley from my house, said she'd sew the patches onto our jackets. The perfect setup, right?

Yeah, it was the perfect setup all right, but not the way any of us were thinking.

We returned from Downtown, chattering on the streetcar the whole way home about how cool those patches were and how great it was gonna be on Monday when we walked into school with our jackets so jacked up.

Mrs. Mills took all of the patches and all of our jackets and went to work. The next day, we all congregated in her backyard and waited for the awesomeness to begin. At last she emerged, but empty-handed.

"Mrs. Mills, didn't you have a chance to sew our patches on?" we asked.

"Oh yeah, they're all finished," she replied.

"Can we go in and get them now?"

"Well, sure guys. But first, that will be five dollars apiece."

Scientists and sociologists have labored for years looking for a way to shut up boisterous preteen boys in the summertime. They obviously had never met Mrs. Mills. I had never been smacked upside the head with a two-by-four before or since, but I could have sworn I was when I got a five-dollar invoice that I didn't know was coming. The sewing job cost more than the patch itself? What in the blue blazes was going on here, Mrs. Mills?

Now remember, this was the summer of 1971, and I was ten. Scraping up the $3.50 for the patch itself, plus streetcar fare Downtown and back, took some ingenuity and initiative, and I was pretty tapped out at that point. Where was I—or any of my similarly broke buddies—going to get another five bucks while our super cool Pirates-patch jackets were being held hostage in the Millses' living room?

She must have seen the crestfallen, ashen, blood-drained looks on our faces. Mrs. Mills did give us our jackets that day but made sure she eventually got the five-dollar fee from each of her customers (or his mom), too. She had a business to run, after all, I suppose. But the experience never left me.

The fancy Latin phrase is *caveat emptor*, or "let the buyer beware." I prefer to think of it as—and as I tell all of my clients—"let's not have any surprises." That's why I almost always agree with my clients on a flat project fee and a clear scope of work for every engagement before it ever begins. That way, they know how to budget and I know what to expect for my cash flow. No surprises.

Because the last thing I want to do is pull a Mrs. Mills on anybody. Jeez.

One Man's Trash

Reality TV hadn't been invented yet. Or it hadn't yet been foisted upon a fetid, pudgy, limp-minded American population, is perhaps a better way to state it. But if it had existed back then, I knew a household that might have garnered its own slow-motion train wreck of a show.

I never even knew their last name, and the only connection came through a friend in a grade above me who was in the same class with one of the sons. They lived in a rickety, narrow old house, perched tenuously on the side of a steep hill, faded and dented and sagging aluminum siding somehow hugging the structure.

It took what seemed to be about a hundred steps to get from the sidewalk to their front porch, but my buddies and I willingly and eagerly made that cardiac climb about once a month.

For a treasure could be found there. A treasure that was ours for the taking. Free money, for minimal effort. In fact, the hermits inside that creepy hillside hideaway were happy to have us make our semi regular visits.

For, you see, those folks drank Pepsi. A lot of Pepsi. Gallons, barrels, rivers of Pepsi.

And they stuck all the empty bottles on the front porch. Scores of bottles, the old classic glass ones with the contours. Each one worth two cents in refunds.

Found money, ours for the simple cost of hauling bags full of empty Pepsi bottles about four blocks. We'd hike up those steps whenever we were broke (which was the natural state of things when you're in sixth grade), clear off that front porch so that you could see all the chipped concrete again, arrive at the neighborhood store, and collect our booty. Oh, the Good & Plentys, red licorice, baseball cards, Bazooka and Bubs Daddy bubble gum, Pixy Stix, Swedish Fish, and gobs of other goodies made it all worthwhile.

Meanwhile, back at Pepsi Central, the mysterious clan kept guzzling pop till the cows came home. In the race to dental decay, looking back on it now, I'd say it was probably a dead heat—us stuffing our faces with penny candy versus them consuming frightening levels of carbonated soda pop.

This recollection bounced into my head recently when the political dustup started over the president's statement that "you didn't build that; somebody else made that happen," referring to the role of government-provided infrastructure in enabling businesses to operate and succeed.

To my mind, it's a silly argument on both sides. Yes, government provides roads and police and fire protection and water and power—all of the things that make commerce safe and possible. But from where does the money come to pay for these governmental functions? From taxpayers, who earn their incomes from businesses, that's where. It's symbiotic, and any claims to exclusivity or superiority on either side are bogus.

To equate it to my boyhood story, the cavity-challenged family who inhaled cartons of Pepsi-Cola and left their empties on the front porch were like the government. They made our entrepreneurial exploits possible. No bottles from them, no dough for us. As we cleared away the mess from their front porch, it helped them get rid of a problem while providing us with revenue. Our little "business" could succeed, and everybody won in the end.

One man's trash is another man's treasure, after all.

The Kroger-Pro Caper

In the late 1970s, things were pretty rough. Double-digit inflation, mortgage rates at 18 percent or higher, long lines where you could buy gasoline only on odd-numbered dates if your license plate ended in an odd number, and vice versa.

From the perspective of a fifty-one-year-old father of three today, it's remarkable and downright admirable how people made it during those bleak economic times, but as a high school student back then, the pains of a dicey economy pretty much rolled off my back.

That was, however, until the night we were first served Kroger-Pro.

My mom shopped at Kroger's supermarket, the store nearest to our house. The Kroger chain used to have a strong presence in western Pennsylvania until a contract dispute with its employees caused the firm to pull up stakes and abandon this market. No one's seen a Kroger's around here for decades.

As a result, I have no idea whether Kroger-Pro is sold anymore. I sure hope not. Because that stuff was nasty. Allow me to explain.

My siblings and I were dyed-in-the-wool carnivores. I know I certainly remain one today. Our mom made wonderful meals. Great Italian dishes of spaghetti with meat sauce, fantastic meatballs, delicious. She still does.

One evening we sat down to enjoy another happy helping of pasta with meat sauce. We dug in, forks feverishly twirling the noodles against big soup spoons, the lip-smacking ground beef doing its job and literally beefing up the meal. We opened our eager mouths, popped in the felicitous forkfuls, and began chewing, taste buds anticipating the traditional dance of delectability. But then the party of the palate came to an abrupt, jarring, screeching halt.

Something was wrong. Very wrong. Calamitously wrong. Did Mom forget how to cook? What is up with this weird meat sauce? We charter members of the Mount Oliver Carnivores Club demanded answers!

She made a cursory sweep of her eyes around the table and knew the jig was up.

"It's Kroger-Pro!" she said, mustering all of the pride and dignity the moment deserved.

"What the heck is Kroger-Pro?" we shot back.

"It's just like ground meat," Mom said.

"Yeah, but what *is* it, Mom? Where's the *real* meat?"

Turned out that Kroger-Pro was a soy-based product. Tofu before tofu was cool, you might say. And a lot less expensive than ground beef in those days.

We finished the meal so as not to have any hurt feelings, but I don't remember many nights featuring Kroger-Pro after that. Mom knew she couldn't blow that jive past us a second time. The beefy expectations of a lifetime had been too successfully ingrained. There was no going back.

I guess the thing I remember most about The Kroger-Pro Caper is the notion that sometimes you're forced to make decisions that can be uncomfortable. Everybody back in 1977 had to live as frugally as possible, our family included. Kroger-Pro offered a more economic alternative to the real thing, so we gave it a shot. In the end, it wasn't the best alternative, so we made other fiscal corrections.

We're in sort of the same economic boat today, all of us. Here's hoping the economy finds its footing again someday soon. Until then, we might have to chew our way through some rough nights of Kroger-Pro. Days of steak will come around again, though. I refuse to believe otherwise.

The Parallels of Pinball

T he last time I swung by the neighborhood where I grew up, the little family-owned store about two blocks from my house had been boarded up and abandoned. And for quite some time, from the looks of it. That made me sad.

In its heyday, this tiny structure—owned and operated for decades by an Italian husband and wife—served as the nerve center of our little slice of the world. For the proprietors, it was not only their means of support, it also was their home, at least on the second floor. For the moms and dads in the neighborhood, it was the place to grab a quart of milk, a little lunch meat, maybe even a pack of smokes. For the civic minded, the basement served as the polling place each Election Day, for crying out loud.

For kids like me, though, it was the place—the only place—to indulge in all of the vices that a bunch of preteen Catholic boys had at our disposal. Penny candy by the pound, which actually sold for a penny. Racks of comic books that we tried to read as far as possible before the owner brought the hammer down and demanded either payment or removal from the premises. Packs of baseball cards that we would trade and flip outside to accumulate as many Pirates as possible from the other guy.

But the centerpiece of it all, the Taj Mahal of our particular kid-dom, the Holy Grail of cheap thrills, was the pinball machine impossibly tucked into a corner of the store. Visible through one of the front pane-glass windows, the pinball machine served as the flame to us moths, burning us appropriately, one quarter at a time, spitting out five silver balls of potential neighborhood glory.

Kids today play video games, the vastly inferior descendants of pinball machines. A video game progresses along a planned sequence of events and escalating challenges. The longer you play a video game, the better you get at it, because you figure out how to beat the scenarios programmed into it. Okay, the realism can be impressive, and you can sure tip your hat to the complexity of the story. But it's not the same as playing pinball.

In pinball, every time you pulled that launch lever back and set that silver ball flying into motion, it was different. It took incredible hand-eye coordination as the pinball would bounce and bang off the stoppers, lights flashing, bells dinging. The pinball would fall into holes in the board, shoot out again, and fly downward to the flippers as the mechanical scoreboard clicked and rang. Getting those flippers to catch the ball at just the right angle and speed to send it back up into the play zone became a gift. Thinking you had it set up just right, only to see the ball drop out of play, even as you frantically pressed those flipper buttons, always teed me off.

The best thing about pinball, though, came back to control. It was a machine. A fairly big machine for a kid. And you had complete control of it, pushing, shaking, cajoling the entire structure to help get that pinball where you wanted it to go. Of course, too much body English applied to the machine got you a "tilt," and the whole game was over. Another 25 cents down the tubes.

You look at the news—or your own life—any day of the week, and the parallels with pinball can be easily made. Every morning people get out of bed and launch their day, and regardless of plans, each day is going to turn out different in some way. You can't predict anything with any certainty. You fly around, bouncing off other people and obligations and commitments and surprises, trying to stay in the game long enough to rack up a decent score without pushing, shaking, or cajoling others so hard that you earn yourself a tilt.

In the end, it's all about control. The "self" kind, mainly, I suppose.

Too bad that old neighborhood store is gone. I had a couple of quarters to spare that day.

The Incredible Mr. Vis

The year was 1970 and I was all of ten years old, one of about forty Cub Scouts sitting on the floor of the local Moose lodge one chilly Friday evening, spellbound by the superlative story-telling of Mr. Vis, one of the troop leaders.

Good gravy, Mr. Vis knew how to spin a tale. Using only his voice and his gestures, he had us Scouts (and our parents) alternatingly in terror or in stitches, crawling through a murky forest or soaring through a golden cloud, taking on a gang of villains or taking off for a new adventure. He did it with such aplomb, zest, and joy that forty years later I can still conjure the experience clearly in my mind.

Faxes didn't exist back then. No e-mail, either. Texting, Facebook, Twitter, or any of the other electronic means to communicate we enjoy (or is it endure?) today would have fallen under the rubric of science fiction when Nixon occupied the White House. Nope, we had the U.S. Postal Service, the Bell Telephone Company, and each other. Those were pretty much the only means of communication.

And I miss those days.

According to a study done by GfK Technology cited in *Fortune for Small Business* magazine, 87 percent of adults today say they prefer dealing with others in person instead of via computers or smart-phones. The same compilation of statistics shows that, according to

Pear Analytics, 62 percent of all Tweets comprise babble or otherwise worthless information.

Of course, social media is here to stay, yet so much of it seems trivial, impersonal, and actually uncommunicative to me. Why does the English language need to fit on a two-inch screen? My guess is that most people have firsthand experience of an e-mail or text message—especially one meant to be funny or sarcastic—being misinterpreted and requiring even more follow-up damage-control communications. That's silly and such a waste of time.

When you're speaking on the phone, or better yet face-to-face with someone, the chances of being properly understood would seem to increase exponentially. When people can hear vocal inflections, read facial expressions, and get a human feel for what's being said, things just work out better.

As a professional writer, I also get concerned about the ability of people to communicate powerful ideas with passion, to build and utilize a robust vocabulary, and to sustain a cogent thought for at least a paragraph or two. Anyone who thinks Tweeting will help along those lines qualifies as a twit in my book.

I overhear young people in my neighborhood debating ways to communicate with their friends, but placing a phone call where they would actually have to speak back and forth with another person rarely even gets considered. That's a damn shame. My bet is, if kids today had been with me and my friends as Mr. Vis wove his amazing stories, they'd feel differently and would look for ways to talk face-to-face more often.

Sleeping Out

In my fifty-plus years on this planet, I've lived in an air-conditioned home for only four or five of those years. Most of the time, it doesn't pose much of an issue. But for a handful of days each summer, the lack of climate-controlled comfort can be a real bear.

This held true at the house where I grew up, as well. The nice thing was, every other house on our block had the same problem. Nobody had air conditioning, so we all sweated and suffered together.

My buddies and I used such sweltering, swampy summer nights to our advantage, though. It was a card we couldn't overplay, but when conditions became ripe, play it we did.

We called it "sleeping out."

The houses on our block all had front porches, where, on the nights our parents said it was okay, we'd bring our sleeping bags to the designated guy's house and all camp out overnight. It wasn't any more or less comfortable than inside the house, necessarily, but somehow the heat and humidity never felt as oppressive while goofing around with your friends after midnight.

The wheedling, bargaining, and outright pleading for the green light to sleep out with friends must have been impressive, because we always seemed to be able to assemble the whole gang for these porch-bound evenings. Either that, or our parents were so eager to get us out of their hair for one night, they'd have said yes on the first try.

We assembled at the designated guy's porch after the streetlights came on, which usually marked the time when we had to come in for the night. We'd play cards, tell stories, and try not to raise enough of a ruckus to bring any parents out onto the porch to check on us. Wasn't much sleeping going on during these "sleeping out" nights.

These adventures went on each summer from about fifth grade until eighth grade, and in those later years we of course became more daring. The furthest we ever pushed the limit came one scorching summer Friday night, when we decided to go AWOL from a friend's porch and walk up the hill to the pizza shop for some slices.

Snickering and laughing, we tugged on our Converse All-Stars, slipped off the porch, and started on our way. Thrilled with a sense of rebellion and high spirits, we burst through the door of the pizza shop and confidently placed our orders. When the kid behind the counter told us how much we owed, however, reality set in.

None of us had brought any money, each assuming the other guy had some. Guess we weren't ready to escape the porch after all.

Chastened, hungry, the boldness slapped out of us by a lack of $3.75, we wended our way back down the hill, back to the abandoned porch full of unfurled sleeping bags and scattered playing cards.

And that's when the headlights found us. Our buddy's dad, the one whose porch we had flown, became alarmed by the lack of noise, realized we were gone, and came looking for us in his Chevy Impala. And good golly gosh, was he a tad upset.

Thus endeth our sleeping-out days—starting that very night as he yelled at us to grab our stuff, get off his porch, and go back home where we belonged. After that came high school, and sleeping out suddenly had lost its cool.

But, man, did we come close to a legendary night. All lost for the sake of $3.75 worth of crummy pizza.

Around and Around and Around

O ne of the most enjoyable toys when I was a kid had only three moving parts: a pen, some plastic pieces, and your brain. Spirograph.

A box full of different plastic discs with teeth around the edges and holes in various spots. You'd line up the disc against an outer frame that also had teeth. You'd let the two sets of teeth mesh, stick the pen in one of the holes, and start moving the disc around and around. Every design turned out different. For a verbal person like me, who revels and delights in words, Spirograph allowed me the illusion that I could be visually artistic, too.

Long before computers did most of the thinking for us, Spirograph challenged the user to imagine a design—or even better, to just start and see how the design would take shape. So simple, so surprising, so much fun. And all from just going around and around and around.

If communication between people could only work the same way. If going around and around and around could only produce something beautiful. Alas, that's not how it works.

Case in point? Heck, pick up the newspaper any day of the week. Pay attention to what comes out of people's mouths, regardless of what the issue might be. From blustering and bloviating testimony before Congress to Lance Armstrong's halfhearted confession to

Oprah. From evasive nonresponses from defense attorneys on local TV news to the claims desk of your favorite insurance company.

Can't anybody just give a straight answer anymore? We go around and around and around, and clarity takes it on the chin.

What's the problem? Is it that people are so afraid of litigation or retaliation that they've decided it's easier to verbally obfuscate? Have we become so skittish about being honest and direct that we're constantly hiding, hoping to run out of the line of fire without being confronted?

I'm as guilty as anyone on this score. In high school, I loved being in the band, and I loved having the respect of the band director. At one point during my senior year, I lost my folder of music. But my convoluted adolescent sense of logic told me not to say anything and to try to play my part by memory, because that folder was bound to pop up any day now.

Naturally, that ruse didn't last more than a couple of days. I was busted, and it tainted the band director's opinion of me for the remainder of my senior year. The fact of that still hurts to this day. And all from going around and around and around, stalling for time, dodging the truth, avoiding facing the music, as it were.

(The folder did turn up a few days later, by the way. A sworn high school enemy had stolen and hidden it. I've truly hated only one or two people in my life. And even though it's some thirty-five years later, that guy remains on the list.)

How much more smoothly would the world spin if we all stopped spinning our messages? Yes, telling the truth can be tough. It makes a mess sometimes. But it also identifies the messes that need to be cleaned up so that we can get on with it and keep going—stronger, more confident, more proud.

Around and around and around. With Spirograph, it made wonderful pictures. But with people, not so much.

Eighty-eight Little Keys

She couldn't have been older than second or third grade when it magically appeared in their house. Made of polished dark wood, with gleaming gold pedals and a playing surface of shining white, just waiting for her. Only her.

So she clambered up onto the padded seat, marveling at this gift, so unexpected, so wonderful, placed her hands on the keys, and started to play. Very simple, rudimentary melodies at that point, but in time this little girl—my mother—would make music on that piano that filled our home, our lives, with memories to treasure.

A George Steck upright model, with a "birdcage" system of hammers and strings inside the body, that piano served as the centerpiece of some great family sing-alongs when all of the aunts, uncles, cousins, and grandparents on my mom's side would come over on a Sunday afternoon. Mom would be on piano, Uncle Ed would bring his banjo, and the rest of us would sing our heads off together. Neighbors be damned, we were having fun making music.

"The Impossible Dream," "Mississippi Mud," "Shine on Harvest Moon," "The Shadow of Your Smile"—we knew them all. In fact, I think I was the only kid in my class who understood the joke when Jane Jetson sang "Won't You Fly Home, Bill Spacely?" on *The Jetsons* because the old standard, "Won't You Come Home, Bill Bailey?" always remained in our family repertoire.

My mom is a great lady, very petite, with smallish hands. How she was able to play some of those chords and songs, where the notes were pretty far apart, baffled and amazed me. If she wasn't exactly breaking the laws of physics, she sure was giving them a hell of a stretch.

As kids, we would tinker around on the keys, trying to figure out that catchy Charlie Brown Christmas song. I'd work on the lower notes, the rhythm, while my sister pecked out the melody. We got it going pretty good a couple of times. Eventually, my sister began taking piano lessons and became quite accomplished herself.

In time, as we left for college and careers, the piano stayed in its designated spot along the wall in the dining room for many years. Not sure how much Mom played it while we were off building our lives, marrying our spouses, populating the family with kids of our own, but I hope it was more often than not.

After a few years, it made more sense for the piano to move to my sister's house. But a few years after that, it came to my house, where my daughters could learn to play in preparation for their music degrees in college. It remains in our family room today, where it still gets played fairly frequently.

The keys might not shine quite so white, the body looking a bit weathered, the pedals worn from years of being pressed. But it still makes the same magical sound it did when that eight-year-old girl discovered it, the gift of a lifetime, a lifetime ago.

When I think of everything that piano has seen and been a part of over the past almost seven decades, it's impressive. All of the family history, the highs and the lows. The endless hours of practicing. Dozens of toddlers smashing the keys to make that big crazy sound. The women of our family, playing, when the house was empty, just for the sheer joy of creating and experiencing music for herself.

And, mostly, when all of us—this wild, wonderful, extended Italian family—would crowd into that tiny dining room to sing old songs at the top of our lungs. As a family. You can't buy that kind of love, a love that has bonded each of us ever since. All it takes is eighty-eight little keys.

Won't you come home again, Bill Bailey? The piano's right here.

Miracles Small and Large

The sun hadn't even begun to sneak a peek over the horizon yet, but under that gauzy, pink-and-beige, pre-sunrise sky, my younger sister and I silently snuck downstairs every Easter morning while everyone else slumbered away.

Looking behind couches, under the piano bench, on top of the fridge, and a dozen other of Mom's reliable hiding places, within seconds we had each found our basket, full of chocolate and marshmallows and jellybeans, resting on plastic "grass" stuffed across the bottom. Breakfast was served!

Next, we'd go over to the giant Sears TV console, adjust the big plastic knob that rotated the antenna up on the roof, and flip channels until we found it. Our favorite Easter morning show. Once it started at 6:30 a.m., we plopped onto the floor, started unwrapping the bunnies and eggs, and watched, riveted to the screen, for the next 30 minutes.

I couldn't even guess the name of the program we liked so much. It starred no one famous. Its production values, if by some miracle I saw it again today, would no doubt be appallingly low and embarrassingly amateur – with the quality of acting not far behind. But we loved it. Easter wasn't Easter until we'd seen it.

The show depicted the story of Christ's crucifixion (which got dispatched right up front, very quickly and neatly) and resurrection (which got the lion's share of screen time). I have no way to explain or justify this, but the image of Peter and John running to the empty tomb and looking in – I see that as clearly and vividly in my mind's eye today as when I was seven.

Images from that little shoestring religious TV show made the Gospel readings in church later that morning so much more relatable. After all, I had just seen those two guys actually do what Father only read about at Mass. It became real in my head, not just a story out of a book.

Isn't it uncanny how little slices of experience and exposure stick with you for decades? Why would a low-budget, half-hour, pious early-morning program about the Easter story not only take on such significance for a little kid, but remain a treasured memory almost a half-century later?

The same thing happened at Christmas every year. I could not get into a holiday spirit, Christmas just wasn't Christmas, until I head Linus quoting the story of the Nativity from the Gospel of Luke during "A Charlie Brown Christmas." In fact, I remember racing home to our newlywed apartment after a school board meeting I had to cover as a newspaper reporter, bursting through the door and flipping on the TV just in time to hear Linus, clutching his blanket, explain, "That's what Christmas is all about, Charlie Brown." It saved my whole season that year.

Today, of course, nobody has to wait for anything to run on TV. You can slip in a DVD or go the iTunes Store and watch whatever, whenever. "Rudolph" on Flag Day? No problem. "The Ten Commandments" at the beach? Why not?

And while I'm all for technology, access, and convenience, I still think there's something to be said for tradition. For appropriateness and association. For waiting until it's the proper time to enjoy things.

Things like the small miracles of growing up that last forever – such as sneaking downstairs with your kid sister in the pre-dawn silence of Easter, munching on chocolate rabbit ears, and watching Peter and John on TV running to the empty tomb, discovering the greatest miracle in history and one that also will last forever.

He is Risen. Happy Easter, everyone.

The Show

Kids today know only megaplex theaters—giant, multiscreen, mall-bound behemoths where patrons get force-fed cold, overpriced, gummy, subpar popcorn on their way to darkened far-flung rooms, some of which (if not hosting a blockbuster feature) could double as indoctrination cells for prisoners of war.

It's a sad, sorry business, if for no other reason than it deprives an entire generation of the full-bodied thrill of walking—yes, walking, with no vehicles required—to enjoy that week's movie at a true neighborhood theater.

We had just such a bijou in the little borough where I spent my youth. Its proper name might have been the Mount Oliver Theater, but we just called it The Show. As in, "You wanna go up The Show?" Or, "What are they showing up The Show today?" Or, "I don't have any money. You think we could sneak into The Show?"

The Show must have really been something in its heyday, long before my lunkhead friends and I would saunter up there to watch movies. It had a gilded, glass-fronted box office right out front along the sidewalk, where typically an older lady took your dough and pumped out your little red perforated ticket.

Every ticket looked the same, just like a raffle ticket. It didn't have the name of the movie, or what "auditorium" it was playing in, or the time of day when purchased, or your zodiac sign, or any one of the thirty-seven other stupid, irrelevant details you get on movie tickets today.

Ticket in hand, you then pulled open the heavy glass doors and walked up the sloped foyer covered in plush red carpeting, through another set of glass doors, and into the main lobby.

Here's where the advantages of having a neighborhood movie theater came to life. Chances were pretty good you knew one of the kids working the refreshment counter, so prices occasionally got curiously overlooked or somehow reduced by a wide percentage.

I had a friend from my homeroom at school who enabled and supported my Nibs habit for years. A favorite of mine, Nibs were thick chunks of sweet red licorice—sheer nirvana, trust me—and getting them for free from a fellow Catholic school co-conspirator? I would submit that life couldn't possibly get any better. I think Mary Ann and I just added that sin to the list we told Father when our eighth-grade class got trooped up the hill to church for confession once a month.

Loaded down with free Nibs and an orange Creamsicle from the freezer vending machine—good God, maybe life actually *could* get better!—you walked through the heavy red curtains that hung from the doorway into the theater itself. And there, my friends, was when you really got spoiled as a movie lover.

The Show probably held three hundred patrons on the main floor and an additional one hundred in the rear balcony, each chair featuring a red velvet back and a well-worn leather seat. Down front highlighted two private boxes—long since out of use—overlooking what had been a stage during vaudeville days. Ornate paintings on the ceiling and around the proscenium—faded and chipped over time—gave the old girl a touch of class. And in front of the screen was an enormous, thick, crimson-with-gold-trim curtain that separated from the center—just like a live performance—when the projector began to click and the feature film of the day began.

There was nothing corporate about The Show, nothing impersonal or cold or off-putting. You went there, and you felt welcomed.

It was our theater, in our neighborhood, where our friends tore the tickets and shoveled the popcorn and ran the projector. From the annual Christmas party for kids—featuring such rich cinematic fare as *Snow White and the Three Stooges* and *A Man Called Flintstone*—to the special prepubescent joy of throwing pieces of Lemonhead candy at the back of other kids' heads seated ten rows ahead of you, and from offering a cool, air-conditioned respite from the heat and humidity of a sweltering summer's day, to the luxury of walking home with your friends, talking about the movie the whole way, The Show helped make our little slice of the city something to look back on now with real appreciation.

The Show connected us as friends and neighbors, just as much as the church or the school or the library or the park or the swimming pool or the little business district did. That's why I find it sad that very few people over the past thirty years or so have ever experienced that communal feeling when going to the movies. It truly was great. Special. Unforgettable.

I know it's a long shot, but hey, Mary Ann, if you're out there, can you sneak me a bag of Nibs for old time's sake?

ST. JOE'S SCHOOL:
Survival in a Parochial Biosphere

For eight years, this cluster of buildings, positioned just down the hill from the parish church, which sat at the highest point in town, served as the host to learning, friendship, laughter, and even a first slow dance with a girl. As long as you didn't actually press up against her, that is. This bastion of Catholic education named for St. Joseph, patron saint of workers, sure worked us hard. But it also gave us a place to grow and develop into students ready to move on.

The Sister Dorothy Mysteries

On a balmy afternoon in June, it felt as if the weight of the world had lifted. A grueling slog had, at last, come to an end. The daily grind of living up to expectations, the mounting pressure—and then, the seemingly unobtainable had finally been obtained.

Kindergarten was over.

No more suffering under the lash of Mrs. Beecher the Teacher. Sweet summer had burst into its full spectrum of Technicolor glory, filling our lungs with its savory scents with every breath, and offering shackle-free, unending sunshiny days with no rules and no limits. The very thought of being in school again—ever—was not to be mentioned, tolerated, or countenanced.

But, of course, like all perfect dreams, this one came to a sudden, solemn end as my next-door neighbor and I made the first of what would be thousands of walks to and from our parish's parochial school. We headed off to first grade to meet our teacher, Sister Dorothy.

I went to the same grade school as my mother, sat in the same wood-and-wrought-iron desks lined up by slats on the floor, with a shelf under the desktop for your books, pencil cases, crayons, and other elementary essentials. These antiques had been around so long that a hole for inkwells remained as part of the desktop. Inkwells!

Initials carved into the wood could be the leftover childhood vandalism of the town's current police chief for all we knew.

The room smelled of floor polish, pencil shavings, and the wax paper around the lunch packers' sandwiches. Ziploc hadn't arrived on the scene yet. A handwritten alphabet rode along the top of the blackboard made of real slate. How did we know this? Because a couple of years in the future, an enraged teacher would use a class clown's noggin to put a crack in one of those slate blackboards. Corporal punishment? Oh, you bet.

Sister Dorothy never became physical with any of her first-graders, though. She wore the full *Sound of Music*-style habit, with just her face sticking out of her veil and wimple and a set of rosary beads hanging from the belt around her long black tunic. But instead of presenting an imposing, fearsome image to my classmates and me, Sister Dorothy exuded warmth and kindness. Her classroom became a safe, comfortable place to start the long, never-ending climb toward deeper knowledge, greater understanding, and unassailable character.

You never could tell from which direction a new intellectual challenge might arrive. One of the first puzzles came when Sister Dorothy told the boys that we could use the lavatory. "Lavatory? What the heck is that?" I thought to myself. "We're only in first grade. Why are they letting us get near chemicals and tubes and stuff? What are we supposed to do in this lavatory?" So, like a good little lemming, I just followed the single-file line into the boy's bathroom, still looking for the chemicals and beakers. What a fun-sized twit.

Then came the day when some fourth-graders came into our room selling cupcakes or something for their class's field-trip fund. We knew this was coming, so most of us came prepared with money. As the older kids wrapped up their little sale, one of them said, "Does anybody need change?"

"Gosh, that's a pretty deep question to ask a bunch of six-year-olds," I again thought to myself. "Yes, we all need change. That's why we're in school, to change and grow and get smarter and all that. But what does that have to do with cupcakes? What am I missing here?" The perfect little Catholic bubble-brain.

The year with Sister Dorothy passed without incident for the most part. Until the day, that is, when somebody didn't quite make it to the lavatory. And I mean *really* didn't make it, in the worst way possible, if you get my drift. Then it was into the cloak room—Can you believe it? The "cloak room," as if we were all wizards attending Hogwarts and wearing our flowing black cloaks!—one at a time, boys first, to identify the guilty party. But anybody cursed enough to be sitting downwind could have saved Sister a lot of trouble on that score, trust me.

When June rolled around again, it became time to say good-bye to Sister Dorothy. The sense of busting through chains and shackles, felt so keenly a year earlier, never happened. We loved Sister Dorothy, and she loved us. Second grade held the specter of another lay teacher, clouding our shared nun-less future. But Sister Dorothy knew just what to say.

"Boys and girls, I want you to enjoy your summer with your families," Sister Dorothy told us as we lined up to march out of the school building for the last time that academic year. "And remember, I will always remember you and pray for you every day."

I'm not sure I've received such a lovely sendoff since.

Blame Me for Boo-Berry

They say Catholic education has begun to enjoy a resurgence across the country today. I hope so, because it sure served me well as a young lad.

That's not to say my little parochial elementary school didn't need to do some breakneck, heavy-handed, guilt-sodden fundraising on a regular basis, however. Because, trust me on this, we certainly did.

It started with the annual Bazaar, a major socio-economic milestone in our neighborhood community, held each February. Here the normally stoic dads of classmates, guys in suits and ties and somber prayerful expressions at Mass, somehow overnight became the most expressive carnival barkers, enticing passers-by to plop down their cash to match the number where the spinning wheel would land. The Bazaar was a happening, baby.

Hundreds of sweaty Catholics, squeezed into a sweltering gymnasium thanks to the chronically unpredictable steam boiler (two settings: Sahara and Broken), plodded numbly past each other, playing games of chance, the fish pond, darts, and buying other moms' funny-tasting cupcakes at the Mothers Club bake sale—all in a communal effort to keep the church and the school running for another year and to give poor Father some peace of mind up at the rectory.

And it didn't end there. In a program that no one in his right mind would conduct today, each pupil received a stack of "chance slips"—long pieces of paper with lines for people to write their name and phone number if they agreed to buy a chance to win the big parish raffle. Chances sold for a dime a line, or a dollar for the whole sheet.

But here's why no one would ever do this today, or ever again. We, the pupils of our elementary school, were expected to go door-to-door and solicit people on our own. Six- and seven-year-old kids knocking on doors, including even the (gasp!) occasional non-Catholic door. Can you imagine the liability today? The parish couldn't possibly sell enough chances to afford the insurance! Back then, though, we lived in a different world. A nicer, safer world in so many ways.

My favorite fundraising activity, though—even if I didn't realize the purpose behind it at the time—came when some fellow second-graders and I got to come to school early every day for a week and eat cereal.

Years later I learned that our merry band of munchers served as part of a national blind taste test for the introduction of Boo-Berry cereal. All we knew was that we had boxes upon boxes of unmarked cereals to pick from, every day for a whole week, and no grown-up would ever say no! Not all children could handle this level of freedom and autonomy at such a tender age, you understand. Yet such was the burden my friends and I carried.

As I recall, Frosted Flakes remained a big hit. The terrible, cardboardy twigs-and-bark brands got ignored, of course. This weird blue one had potential, though. It was plenty sweet, I knew that for sure.

Being educated by nuns, and lay teachers who thought just like nuns, we knew always to be polite and give a nice response to our elders. Or else. That's probably why all the reviews we gave to the people with clipboards were positive, no matter if we thought their funky blue cereal tasted like corn syrup-coated crap. Which, of course, it was and still is.

Preservatives and sugar be damned! We were sacrificing our digestive systems for the parish, doggone it! General Mills kicks a few bucks to the school in return for a week of free cereal tasting—all you could eat and no questions asked, no less. Such a sacrifice. But, hey—you're welcome.

Boy Victim Of Hit-Run

A Mount Oliver boy was reported in guarded condition last night in Mercy Hospital as the result of a hit-and-run accident yesterday near St. Joseph School in Mount Oliver.

Police said Timothy Hayes, 13, of 518 Giffin St., was struck by a green and white car in an alley behind the school about 3 p. m. yesterday. Police said the car was driven by a man and also occupied by a female passenger.

Dear Coward in the Cadillac

ear Coward in the Cadillac,
You won't remember my face, I'm sure, but if you saw me today the same way you did on that March afternoon in 1974—as I sailed fifteen feet into the air after being launched by the front end of your speeding green Caddy—it might sufficiently jog your memory.

Yeah, I'm that kid you hit that day as I walked to my safety patrol post. Ironic, right? On the way to help other elementary school children cross the street safely, I'm the one who takes it on the chops. And you really made a nice, clean hit, too. Let me tell you about it, since your recollection of the event must be minimal.

Patrol boys like me got to leave ten minutes before the rest of the student body to get to our posts on various street corners around the school. An alley ran behind the school building that normally got barricaded on both ends with wooden horses, but the janitor hadn't taken care of that detail yet on our special day, leaving the alley open for traffic as an irresistible shortcut, am I right?

As I walked down an outdoor set of concrete steps and turned the corner of the school building onto the alley, there you were, racing your Cadillac down the narrow blacktop lane. Gosh, you must have been doing forty-five miles an hour if you were doing five.

The impact occurred so suddenly—your timing impeccable, congratulations!—that your front bumper slammed into my left thigh as soon as I cleared the corner of the building. I still have a small dent in the side of my left leg to this day. No wonder I think of you often, Mystery Man, more than forty years later.

The aforementioned janitor was cleaning up a room on the first floor, and looking out the window, horrified, he saw everything that happened next:

1) I flew fifteen feet upward and fifteen feet down the alley.
2) I landed on my head and suffered a cracked skull.
3) Blood was coming out of my ears.
4) You slammed on your brakes and then pulled the *coup de grace* of this entire episode.
5) You threw that Caddy into reverse and fled the scene, never to be found, identified, arrested, prosecuted, fined, or incarcerated.

After three days in a coma, my brain slowly, softly, swimmingly floated back into somewhat of a normal consciousness. They say your mind is smarter than your brain sometimes, and I believe it, because I have no sentient recollection of being struck, or lying on the pavement, or the chaotic scene that must have descended around me as the rest of the school let out for the day and saw me sprawled, unconscious, in a pool of my own blood.

But, hey, it got my name into the newspaper for the first time! As an aspiring journalist, that had to count for something. Not quite a byline, but baby steps, you know?

My point in writing this letter to you, whoever you are (or were), is to let you know that, despite your best effort to leave me for dead, I made it. With the help of an incredible family and supportive friends—you should have seen the welcome-back party they threw for me in my eighth-grade class about three weeks later—I went on to high school and had a great time there. Next came college and, on the second day of freshman orientation—the second day!—meeting the girl I've been married to now for thirty-five years. We've raised a family that makes me so proud I could bust on a daily basis.

I suppose what I'd like for you to most clearly understand is simply this. That I won. And that you lost.

If any cosmic justice exists, I hope that the despicable, cowardly, inexcusable act you committed that day—not even so much that you hit me but that you ran away and left me there—has haunted your dreams every night for the past four decades. Or, on the other hand, I hope that remorse and guilt have led you to become a more responsible, accountable, upright person. Either option's okay with me, frankly.

My heart and my faith command me to forgive. Then I reach down and feel the forty-plus-year-old dent in my left leg, and forgiveness remains a challenge. Still trying, though.

Surviving and thriving, I remain ...

Tim Hayes

Eight Wheels and the All-Skate

There we stood, my buddies and I and about sixty other kids, on the corner in front of the elementary school on a Saturday evening in January, somewhere around 1971 or '72. Shivering, stomping our feet on the pavement to keep warm, our breath wafting out as steamy billows hitting the frigid air, while we waited most impatiently for that rickety old bus to arrive.

At last somebody shouted, "I hear it!" And it, at long last, appeared. An old school bus, painted red, white, and black, with big block letters on the side: Bethel Roller Rink—Roller Skate ... It's Great!

The roller-skating party had begun. A twice-a-year treat for the kids in my community where we got transported what felt like the whole way across town (now I know it was only about eight miles from my house) and left unattended for four hours of nonstop roller skating, boy-girl drama and befuddlement, lousy cold pizza, and the ever-present risk of public humiliation on a grand scale.

Only in America. We loved it.

In the run-up to the skating party, we'd try to find our mojo, strapping on those metal-clip roller skates that attached to the bottoms of our Converse All-Stars. We'd put on our gear and work on our moves in the front street—a hillside with about a twenty-degree pitch. Skating up the hill? No sweat. Skating down the hill? Starting out was no problem. Stopping, on the other hand—well, at least we got good practice falling down.

Once on the bus, the temperature didn't change much. We still froze, but at least the scream-singing for the next half hour took our minds off it. "Three Cheers for the Bus Driver," always a hit. "Ninety-nine Bottles of Beer on the Wall" lasted for about twenty bottles. Road rage might have been born on those skating party buses now that I think of it. The driver, seething, disappeared into a nearby tavern for some well-earned self-medication while we all ran into the rink.

You got your skates and started lacing them up. These were the good kind—black leather for the guys, white for the girls. Four wheels on each skate, with that big knob in front to help you stop. The big time, my friends. You put on those skates, and suddenly you were Somebody.

Then you stood up and immediately fell on your butt. And you hadn't even set skate on the actual rink yet. Oh, you still were Somebody, all right. Somebody Flat on His Ass, that is.

My personal survival technique called for a slow workup to the real action in the center of the counterclockwise circle of skaters. At first the railings along the outer walls got hugged pretty hard while I got my legs under me and figured out how to turn left for the next 240 minutes. Eventually confidence would build and I could fake it enough to skate near the big dogs in the middle.

All-Skate, of course, was every guy's favorite, but the girls seemed a little more partial to the Ladies Choice announcement for some reason. At age eleven, the very notion of holding a girl's hand while trying not to wipe out and drag her crashing down to the hardwood with me sounded like way too much responsibility. So as the announcer smoothly intoned, "Ladies Choice," I'd go and take a leak in the men's room. I know, what a little chickenshit. But hey, I did it while on roller skates. Doesn't that count for something?

The most fascinating person on the floor, however, had to be Willie. Willie worked there and served as a combination cop-bouncer-referee-and-all-around-showoff. The man could roller-skate like an Olympian. The problem was, he knew it. We admired him. We emulated him. We hated him.

In his crisp, white security guard shirt and patrolman's hat, Willie ran the limbo contest, tooting his whistle in grandiose fashion if you touched the floor or knocked off the stick. Willie policed the hokey pokey, charging over and getting in your face if you didn't put your right foot in or out on cue. Willie escorted any hooligans off the floor and scared the rest of us out of our wits, barreling down on us from behind and zooming by so fast it made your hair flutter in his back draft. What a skater. What an authority figure. What a jerk.

A roller-skating party promised four hours of bumps and bruises, sore ankles, stomachaches, the flames of romance blazing like the sun then snuffed into charred remains in record time—and some of the craziest, wildest, most joyous fun any of us would ever have. Ever.

Later that night, as the bucket-of-bolts bus dumped us back at the school, our dads came around and drove us home. We had Sunday to relive it all again in our heads, and when Monday morning rolled around and classes began, the nuns knew they didn't stand a chance of teaching us anything at least until after lunch.

Sister, don't you know? We'd been to another legendary roller-skating party last weekend.

Field of Screams

Making a living as a self-employed entrepreneur has its advantages. Freedom, variety, exciting engagements, continually keeping abject terror at bay, to name just a few. But ranking near the top, for me anyway, comes the dress code.

When with clients, of course, it's business appropriate. But when working from my home office, it's comfortable all the way. If the day has no call for dress shirts, pants, and shoes, then it's cotton shirts, jeans, and tennies.

The realization came to me recently as to why I think of business attire as a need-only option: eight years of Catholic education.

Every day for eight years, guys like me wore dress shirts, dress pants, and dress shoes to school. The only exception came during seventh and eighth grades, when we could wear jeans one Friday each month because we got bused to shop class, run by the Pittsburgh Public Schools. Other than that, we looked like little businessmen, traipsing by foot to school in the morning, back home for lunch, back to school again, and home after 3 p.m.

And perhaps the craziest part of all this came during the twenty-five minutes or so between the moment we arrived back at school after eating lunch at home and when the bell rang to start afternoon classes. Why, you ask?

Because that's when the entire student population—from first through eighth grade, guys in shirts, slacks, and penny loafers; girls in blouses, skirts, and Mary Janes—ran amuck on the "playground." A term used extremely loosely because our playground consisted of an asphalt half acre—on a slant, no less—bordered by a cyclone fence and two brick walls.

You ever try to play tag on a slanted field of asphalt? The opportunities for mayhem, injury, and lifelong scars—both physical and emotional—ran high. The only patch of grass anywhere near the school or the adjoining church surrounded the rectory, and Father wanted none of this nonsense outside his window. Looking back now, can't say I blame him.

The school provided no balls, no painted hopscotch or four-square diagrams, no basketball hoops, no benches, and damn near no supervision. Think *Lord of the Flies* with about three hundred preteen kids running wild in business clothes. If nothing else, it sure as hell toughened us up for high school.

The trick for me came in sticking close to a small group of like-minded guys who didn't like conflict or contact. We'd just sit off to the side and tell jokes or trade baseball cards. Peaceful coexistence, like those bumper stickers with all the religious symbols, you know? Even though we obviously were all Catholics in this instance.

Every now and then, though, we got corralled into a game organized by the class bullies—with red rover the pinnacle of bulliosity. Gosh, I hated that game. Two teams, with one team forming a long line by holding hands side-by-side. You called out a challenge to the other team, shouting, "Red rover, red rover, dare send Timmy over!" Then, that poor victim had to run at full speed at the other team's line and try to break through one of the hand-holding links in the human chain.

A vicious game, after which you were virtually guaranteed to file back into school with either a gash on your face, a ripped pair of pants to go with your scraped and bleeding knees, or a really sore arm and a possible dislocated shoulder. As the runner, you faced one of three scenarios. One, you broke through the line successfully, which meant you got to join the smug cadre of hand-holders. Two, you failed to break through, which sent you back into the pile of teeth-chattering rabble to await the next dare. Or three, the kids you tried to break through let their hands go just as you braced for impact, and you went sprawling, spoons over teacups, across the black tar.

Red rover, played on an asphalt hill in shoes not built for running, made for some memorable childhood moments. As hard as one might try to forget them. No wonder the bullies loved it.

So today? Yeah, it's jeans and tennies whenever possible, baby. That way, if the neighbors want to start a pickup game of red rover, at least I'll have the right equipment and a fighting chance.

Nuns Can Be Groovy, Too

Over the course of my elementary education, I sure met a lot of sisters. The kind with habits. And veils. And rosary beads. And an approach to discipline that certainly felt unshakable, unalterable, and unbelievable to me and my fellow disciplinees along the way.

Sister Dorothy, Sister James Ann, Sister Esther, Sister Joachim, Sister Frederick—we crossed paths with them all in our eight glorious years at dear old St. Joseph School. The school's no longer standing, and even the parish has been subsumed into a merged conglomerate of Catholics. Kind of sad, really. All those students over all those years, creating all those memories. And that's all they are now, just memories.

Most of those recollections remain positive and happy, whether a matter of selective amnesia or not. As with anybody, some rough days happened, of course. But they fell into the minority of experiences.

One teacher stood out from all the rest, though. A teacher who really "got" the kids in her class. Who ran a tight ship, but also a fun ship. She loved her job, loved her faith, and loved her students. And we loved her back.

My fifth-grade teacher, Sister Ruth Ann. The grooviest nun I ever met, or ever would meet. She was a lot younger than most of the other nuns at St. Joe's. She wore a black veil and dress, but the dress came to her knees, not the floor-length habits the others wore. And if Sister Ruth Ann had a rosary on her, we never saw it.

Remember now, when kids hit fifth grade, they're starting not to be kids anymore. It's a weird time. The first whiff of hormones gets carried on the breeze. Girls begin to cluster and get mysterious and moody. Guys assume more of a young-buck attitude. It's not full-blown adolescence, with its accompanying pain-in-the-arse drama and trauma, just yet. But it's peeking over the back fence in fifth grade.

Sister Ruth Ann understood this and created a classroom environment where learning—for the first time in our academic careers—took on less of a lecturing flavor and more of a participatory slant. She had us up and out of our cast-iron and wooden desks every day. She instituted class officers and activities, with yours truly winning election as vice president, the safest job (or so I thought). She even took us outside for classes, which might have been an excommunicable offense in 1971. I'd have to check canon law on that one.

I can remember Sister Ruth Ann helping us to plan a class party to celebrate some collective achievement, whatever it was. Knowing that a party stood at the end of whatever instructional path she had us on absolutely did the trick in getting our class—even the deadwood delinquents who never seemed to catch on—motivated, working together, and enjoying our school time together.

When the classmate in charge of bringing a stack of 45s to provide the music for the party really dropped the ball, showing up with "Sugar, Sugar" by the Archies—and nothing else—it didn't matter. Sister Ruth Ann danced along with us as those three minutes of pure bubblegum played over and over. We had a blast. She was so cool.

Late in our fifth-grade year, Sister Ruth Ann's brother passed away unexpectedly. The class voted that its vice president should represent the group at the funeral, which I was sort of terrified to do. But when it came to helping Sister Ruth Ann during a sad time, one rose to the occasion as class vice president, no questions asked.

I have no idea where Sister Ruth Ann is today. Truth be told, I couldn't even tell you her last name. But wherever she is, I hope she's loving life the same way she did way back when, with her veil swaying, eyes smiling, dancing to "Sugar, Sugar," having a ball, and proving that nuns could be groovy, too.

The Binary System

In seventh grade, it becomes increasingly difficult to stand apart from the crowd, other than when bullies taunt certain kids, making them stand out in ways they'd rather avoid. Our seventh-grade class at St. Joseph School abided by these cruel and crushing rules of budding adolescence, just as strongly as any public school, let me tell you.

Yet somehow I managed to stand out in a positive way—even if only for a fleeting moment—when I wrote my masterpiece. My Sistine Chapel. My *Pieta*. My *Mona Lisa*. My Newton's first law of motion. My E=mc2, for gosh sakes.

"The Binary System." A fifteen-minute presentation researched, written, and delivered as my entry into the Pennsylvania Junior Academy of Science competition. A thing of beauty. Binary beauty, that is.

For those keeping score at home, the binary system refers to the series of 1s and 0s used in digital technology, with 1 and 0 the simplest possible method available. How I stretched that single fact into fifteen glorious minutes, I couldn't tell you. But somehow I did, delivering my presentation in front of a bunch of unfamiliar science teachers in a school building about seventy-five miles from my house. For whatever reason, that morning I was in the zone, rattling off points like nobody's business, even handling the Q&A like a pro—and won a first-place medal at the regional competition for my trouble.

History is littered with luminaries who rose to fame too quickly and plummeted back to earth, torn to ribbons, flaming out in spectacular fashion. Ah, the heady times at St. Joe's that following week as a once moderately popular nerdnik attracted the spotlight. Adulation can be quite the intoxicating muse if memory serves.

I should have seen the crash coming, though. As a regional first-place winner, the next phase would come a month later at the state competition, held that year in—wait for it—Erie. Yes, folks, he said Erie. The Erie, Pennsylvania, of today might be a clean, wonderful spot to live, visit, and vacation. The Erie, Pennsylvania, of 1973, however? Uh, not so much.

My parents and I drove up the night before and stayed in a local motel because my presentation had been scheduled for the morning session. A girl from my class had also won top regional honors, and she and her dad came up, too. The next morning, a Saturday, I got dropped off at a large, dark, cavernous parochial school with too many floors and too many confusing hallways.

Finding the room where my binary system manifesto was to be declared once more, I sat in the hall with the other hotshots from all over Pennsylvania. When my turn arrived, I entered the classroom and instantly lost my mojo. The presentation went down the tubes in a hurry. I got my facts out of sequence, felt completely at sea during the Q&A, did the big choke, and ended up with a stinking honorable mention. Humbling doesn't begin to describe it.

But the day got even worse immediately afterward when my parents weren't at the front of the school to pick me up. I walked all over that school building, getting disoriented, seeing the other kids driving away with their folks. I finally flagged a nun, a woman who had dedicated her life to the Lord and who told me in no uncertain terms to "Toughen up. Your parents wouldn't leave you here!" Heavens, thank goodness you showed up, Sister. Thanks so much.

They finally did arrive again, about an hour after everything had ended at the school. Turns out my classmate's father, an old high school friend of my parents, suggested that they go see his campground while we were doing our presentations. He promised that this campground was just a couple of minutes away. Yeah, right. More like over an hour. Each way. I thought my mother was going to kill that guy. She would have had to get in line behind me.

Friends, few things in life can beat, for instant depression, a long drive home on a dreary winter afternoon, glaring at an honorable-mention certificate from the Junior Academy of Science, knowing that you choked and that your parents had been hoodwinked, leaving you alone in Erie, Pennsylvania.

It's as simple as 1 and 0.

The Hozzleberry Rosary

E very now and then, you just get skunked. With no time for adequate preparation, you end up improvising, making do with what's on hand. Occasionally you get lucky and it works out, but most times the resulting lack of quality pretty much matches the lack of foresight and forethought.

This dictum holds true in business, government, families, relationships, and—recalling one rather memorable instance—even in an otherwise harmless classroom assignment.

Somewhere around the midpoint of my eight years of Catholic grade school education, Sister gave us a rather interesting project to complete for homework. She granted a two-week period in which to get the thing done, so you knew this was going to require some planning and careful execution.

The assignment? To build a complete rosary using anything we wanted for the beads. That didn't sound so tough.

As background, a Roman Catholic rosary—derived from the Latin term for *ring of roses*—has been used for centuries to help believers pray and meditate on events from the Gospel. It has fifty-nine beads and a crucifix, arranged in a set order, each representing a prayer to be said in sequence until the rosary has been completed.

As standard-issue, ten-year-old American boys at the time, my buddies and I got the assignment from Sister, went home from school, and promptly and completely forgot about it.

Forgot about it until the Sunday afternoon when, while playing touch football in the field behind the houses in our neighborhood, one of us Geniuses for Jesus remembered that Sister expected to collect our homemade rosaries the next morning, that is. At which point we scattered in panic, each Goomba of the Gospel left to his own devices in creating this last-minute masterpiece.

Running toward a neighbor's backyard gate—cutting through the yard representing the quickest way to my house—I stopped to look at the tree just next to the fence. We had climbed this tree countless times, but I viewed it this day in an entirely new way.

The tree grew red berries of some sort. You couldn't eat them, a lesson we had learned the hard way. They carried sort of a strange, bitter smell, as well. We called them hozzleberries. Don't ask me why; I couldn't tell you. The name just seemed to fit, is all.

Scads of them hung on scores of branches above me, and at the time of year this adventure happened, the hozzleberries looked nice and firm. Certainly I could harvest fifty-nine of them and find a way to string them together to make my all-natural, environmentally friendly rosary. A couple of Popsicle sticks for the crucifix, and I'd be golden, baby.

And best of all, it would blow Sister's doors off Monday morning. I'd be the talk of St. Joe's School for weeks.

Five hours, an unbelievable and unwashable red-stained mess, and a hell of lot more than fifty-nine hozzleberries later—the thing finally got finished. I dumped the hozzleberry rosary into a Kroger's grocery paper bag, rolled the top of the bag to close it up tight, and went to bed.

Monday morning as I took my seat, sealed-up Kroger's bag on the floor beside me, little did I suspect the bedlam soon to be unleashed. Sister asked each student to stand up, display his or her rosary, describe the material used for the beads, and explain why that material had been chosen. As I glistened with eager expectation, at last my big moment had arrived.

As I picked up that Kroger's bag, I noticed a huge stain across the bottom. When I opened it, the reason instantly became apparent to the thirty-plus Catholic children and lone adult in that room. The hozzleberries had fermented overnight, decomposing with alarming speed. My awesome rosary had turned into something you wanted to take out behind the barn and shoot in the head. The stink became suffocating. The punishment of Sodom and Gomorrah come to life in a Pittsburgh parochial school classroom! Sister instructed me to immediately take my project down to the basement incinerator for proper burial.

It blew Sister's doors off, all right. And they sure were talking about me in the halls of St. Joe's for weeks. Neither of which occurring in quite the way I had envisioned, obviously.

Moral of the story? Prepare, prepare, prepare. And, by all means, leave those hozzleberries be, up in a tree.

Dustpan

A fter six years of Catholic education, one learns that some things never change. The playground will always be made of asphalt. Up at the rectory, Father will always be shy one healthy sense of humor. And the dress code will always be business casual: blouses and skirts for the girls and dress shirt, slacks, and shoes for the guys.

But as the seventh year dawned, a golden ray of hope, a sliver of delicious possibility, a whiff of sweet deliverance, began to wash over us, tantalizingly teasing the chance to break free of at least one of our unbreakable truths.

Once a month, for Friday afternoon shop class, we rode a bus to a building about two miles away, operated by the city's public school district, to learn about different types of jobs and trade skills. And, as if that weren't a deep enough dive away from our dark parochial classrooms into the milky froth of liberation, here came the true *piece de resistance*: We could wear jeans and tennis shoes!

Oh, shop class! The joy, the celebration, one Friday afternoon a month! And we got to do it during our eighth-grade year, too!

The building housing shop class had two floors where we could sign up for the various subject areas. Things like merchandising, where you got to run a store and operate the cash register; or wood shop, where you got to use a jigsaw to create pieces from blocks of wood; or design, where you could make your own silk-screened T-shirts; and so many more.

My St. Joe's School compadres and I felt like kids with empty bellies and full wallets turned loose in a candy store. Limitless possibilities. Teachers so much cooler than the ones we had. Subjects so far afield of our standard diocesan curriculum that we could hardly believe our good fortune.

I tried to squeeze as much fun and enjoyment out of shop class as possible, naturally. One subject area, though, gave me more satisfaction than any other, and it's an area that I still, to this day, can't believe I did so well in.

Metal shop.

Anyone who knows me, even a little, can validate that my skills as a craftsman leave quite a bit to be desired, to put it mildly. My success in metal shop as a thirteen-year-old kid may never be explained by historians. It promises to perplex the great minds of our time for decades to come. I believe I peaked, some forty-odd years ago, in this regard. Allow me to explain.

The task at hand was to form a small dustpan out of a single flat sheet of black metal. The teacher gave us the materials, measurements, and instructions. At that point, the success or failure of the project fell to each young teenager in that class.

Somehow, with the muses of minor metal crafting smiling down on me, I managed to cut, bend, and solder my hunk of sheet metal into a perfectly formed, completely watertight, fully functional mini dustpan. It felt like a miracle. Me, old fumble-fingers, having created this work of industrial art. If anyone required proof that there is a God, they needed to look no further than that metal shop that day.

The only logical explanation I have ever come up with, that makes any sense at all, is that I attended St. Joseph School—and St. Joseph is the patron saint of craftsmen. That's all I got, folks, and that's what I'm sticking with.

Riding that school bus back to St. Joe's that afternoon, admiring my awesome dustpan, the world seemed a little brighter. Busting down doors you never expected to can be extremely fulfilling.

That dustpan got put to use a time or two in my house, mostly to humor me, I realize now. But at the time, it worked like a charm, and I got the satisfaction of seeing other people get some benefit from something I had created. It's a feeling I still enjoy, but now from providing writing and other communications services. That positive vibe never gets old, never loses its power and punch, let me tell you.

The dustpan triumph of 1973. And it happened while wearing jeans and tennis shoes. Can life get any better? Doubtful, gang. Doubtful.

'The Winner' from Sears

When you're in sixth grade, comparisons count.

Among my fellow classmates at St. Joseph School, circa 1972, especially the other guys, footwear somehow became a critical barometer of status and coolness. We were starting to embark on the road of impressing girls, with all of the misfires and ridiculous ideas that entails in those early stages. But at that point, it remained more important to avoid being labeled a slow goofball among the other young bucks in the pride.

Which, for me, meant acquiring a pair of sneakers that stood above all others as the epitome of cool. They were called "The Winner," and you could get them only at Sears, Roebuck & Co.

Garishly orange with two black vertical racing stripes on the sides, The Winner somehow captured everything a twelve-year-old boy from a solid middle-class family wanted to show the world. Style, suaveness, and speed, all wrapped around your two feet. Unavoidably cool. The kind of shoe Greg Brady would wear. Maybe even Keith Partridge. Yeah.

I can recall hounding my mother about these shoes. How great they were. How much I liked them, needed them even. Plus, we were being hauled to Sears every August anyway to do our school shopping, my two sisters and me, so what was one more purchase in the shoe department? Pleeeeeeeaase!

Eventually, the great day came. We motored out to our familiar Sears store, and after getting fitted with "good pants" and a couple of "good shirts," I was steered into the shoe department, and there they were. Displayed prominently at the entrance of the footwear paradise. The Winner. I can still see them in my mind's eye today, along with the feeling of having my fondest wish finally within my grasp.

The sales guy, with his slightly wrinkled rayon dress shirt and mile-wide necktie (this was 1972, after all), glanced at the clock on the wall (it was fifteen minutes to closing time), sighed heavily, and began the dance. Off came my old Chuck Taylor All-Stars, an inexplicably legendary sneaker that always hurt my feet somehow. He got my size and foot width on one of those big metal things with the sliders on them. And when he asked the magic question, I was ready.

"What kind of shoe do you want, young man?"

"The Winner! Just like that one on the rack over there!" I cried, nearly levitating off the frayed Naugahyde chair with excitement.

My enthusiastic answer might have been met with a barely perceptible eye roll. I can't be sure. But you could only imagine how many times that poor guy had dealt with overeager teenage boys panting over that model in the run-up to the first day of school.

He emerged from the stockroom. Holy cow, even the box was cool! He laced them up, slid them on, tied up the laces, and told me to take the obligatory walk around. Screw that, I was running! They lived up to even my outsized expectations, and my mom forked over the dough. Nirvana in a size ten.

I pounded those Winners into the ground that year. By the time I tossed them into the garbage, you couldn't even tell they were once orange. But in the forty years since I first put them on, I've never told a soul one secret about those shoes. The tennies I lobbied for so heavily. The sneakers I knew would keep me among the cool guys at St. Joe's. The ones I was convinced would eventually get me noticed among the girls.

Gosh, those shoes hurt my feet.

Oh, and one more secret. I'm glad I'm not in sixth grade anymore.

The Wise Potato Chip Guy

The kids just roll their eyes when I pull this old chestnut out of storage. "When I went to elementary school, we had to walk there in the morning, walk home for lunch, walk back to school, and walk home again."

Occasionally I throw in little sweeteners to embellish this heart-tugging tale of hardship and woe, like it was uphill both ways, or we were chased by wild dogs every other day, or some other detail to make it more empathetic. But forget empathetic. My kids just think it's plain old pathetic.

And, truth is, even though my friends and I did make the trek back and forth between school and home twice each day, I remember it fondly. That's how we got to be such good friends, spending fifteen minutes four times a day walking along, talking, joking, throwing snowballs at each other in January and baseballs to each other in May.

And hoping we'd bump into the Wise Potato Chip Guy.

He earned that moniker not necessarily because he was such an impressive intellect, but because he drove a delivery truck for the Wise Potato Chip Company and would stop on random days at a little family-owned neighborhood store we'd pass—long before the days of 7-Elevens.

The definition of a great day for my buddies and me back then? A day when we timed it just right as the Wise Potato Chip Guy unloaded a delivery at the store while we headed back to school after eating lunch at home. He'd see us coming, reach into the truck, pull out a handful of little potato chip bags that maybe had been smashed a little, or that he wasn't worried about accounting for, and toss them to us. We'd thank him, chat him up for a few seconds, and continue on our return trip to school happily munching on some free chips and pretzels and cheese curls.

What motivated the Wise Potato Chip Guy's generosity? Hey, it didn't matter to us; to a bunch of boys heading back to parochial school, this became our version of manna from heaven.

It just goes to show that inspiration, or grace, or just plain good luck can appear from anywhere and at any time. The trick is to be open to it, accept it for what it is, and be thankful. For writers, a perfect phrase pops into your brain as soon as you stop thinking so hard about it. For public speakers, the perfect anecdote to illustrate a point comes zooming out of nowhere to wow an audience and boost your confidence.

Hey, it doesn't matter how it happens. Being receptive to the phenomenon, even expecting it, certainly helps. Maybe that generous potato chip guy was more wise than we ever gave him credit for being, after all.

Wheeler

School is a jungle. Whether growing up in the city or suburbs or rural routes, friendships can be tenuous, threats can spring up like crabgrass, and life carries no promises of calm, peace, or justice. Those ideals can get crushed to powder like a dead brown leaf on a chilly October sidewalk.

That's why it paid to live near Wheeler.

Wheeler—so named because of his propensity for, and mastery of, popping spectacular, long-lasting wheelies on his bike—could outshine anybody on the block when it came to athletic ability. A little on the wild side, Wheeler represented the closest any of the fellow parochial school males on the street would get to living with a spirit of anarchy and contempt of authority. The halo effect of Wheeler's attitude felt simultaneously thrilling and worrisome, like getting away with something really juicy, yet knowing that the terrible swift sword of parental sentencing was ever on the backswing, ready to come down with a vengeance on your ungrateful, smart-alecky neck.

As was wont to happen when more than two boys were forced to gather in one place—like sixth grade, for instance—one of the class bullies started in on a pacifist across the asphalt playground one lunchtime, complaining loudly about some manufactured slight. This alleged—and totally groundless—insult had to be met with two-fisted justice after school, the bully shouted. The truth, however, amounted to nothing more than the sociopathic need for this preteen Cro-Magnon to pound on an easy victim before a rapt audience. Jungle, remember?

The scheduled recipient of this unwarranted beat-down, as we filed back into school for the afternoon countdown to Armageddon, got pulled aside by Wheeler, a neighbor and friend, who said not to worry about any fight. "If the jerk wants to beat you up," Wheeler said, "he'll have to get through me first." The fight never came off as advertised. The fight never came off at all. Wheeler saved the day.

Too bad Wheeler's life inside his own home never reached the heights of his exploits of fearlessness, loyalty, and just plain bad-assery in public. Born second, he fought endlessly to come even remotely close to the reputation of his older brother, who shone like the fire of seven suns in his parents' eyes, but without success. Never good enough, never smart enough, never quite enough no matter what the criteria, Wheeler spent most of his time away from the house the older he got. And that's how it began.

In the 1970s, finding ways to get into trouble in the inner city was no trouble at all. At one of those crucial forks in the road while growing up—where you can choose to be a productive, contributing member of society or not—Wheeler made a bad choice.

As the neighborhood guys started getting into high school activities and expanding their network of friends beyond the home block, Wheeler did even more poorly in class and in finding acceptance and camaraderie—or so it felt, at least. He hung out at the corner store and got into alcohol and drugs, even petty crime, fencing stolen goods to pay for his habit.

Personal counseling, substance-abuse treatment, hospitalized detox stays, spiritual support from the parish priest, even serving as an usher at the wedding of the guy he saved from getting beat up in grade school—all got pursued. None proved effective.

Finally, one early morning, an ambulance from the county coroner's office carried the lifeless body of Wheeler away from his childhood home for the last time, the victim of an accidental overdose, completely alone, in his attic bedroom. He had been up there, dead, for hours before being discovered.

Wheelers exist everywhere. They have great skills. They start out with big hearts. They want to be loved and respected and embraced and accepted, and they deserve it. The Wheelers of the world might feel as if they have no other choice but to seek those things *from* things, like drugs, if they can't get them from people. That's the tragedy.

We are placed on this stupid spinning rock in the middle of blackest outer space for one purpose: to help each other. Wheeler knew that. His after-school defense of a friend facing an unfair fight proved it. It remains a shocking verdict, as he never felt that spirit reciprocated in his life, that it ultimately took his life. And way, way too soon.

Let's do a better job of seeing the Wheelers where we live and work and worship. Let them know we see them. Let them know they're not alone, and that they are valued. It could be the most heroic thing we'll ever do.

Wilson Face-Plant

The secret of life comes in discovering your limitations. Once you get those guardrails in place—as long as you respect them—things generally become easier, smoother, even less painful.

And trust me, I know from whence I speak.

In what could only be described as a well-intentioned, but ill-fated, attempt at increasing the physical fitness of children at our little parochial elementary school—begun at the insistence of one of the younger nuns, still carrying the torch for the fallen President Kennedy, I would guess—everybody in our sixth-grade class was to get hauled down to the school gym once a week for about a month's trial run.

While the chance to get out of our usual business-casual wardrobes and into T-shirts, gym shorts, and tennis shoes came as a rare treat during the school day, the very thought of trying to keep up with the natural jocks sent a chill down the spines of my friends and myself. We were used to goofing around at the neighborhood park, where we played pickup games and displayed uniformly bad skills and the rules somehow didn't count.

Now, in front of everybody in our grade—including the girls—the countdown to soul-crushing, image-shattering, self-worth-pulverizing exposure as clumsy louts on the basketball court had begun.

Sister James Ann picked two captains—the star players, naturally—and they proceeded to select their squads. With each name called that wasn't mine, I could feel the embarrassment building. At least I got shuffled onto one of the teams before the very last kid was chosen.

Clearly second-string material, I rode the bench for most of the class. But good citizenship and sportsmanship—if not necessarily smart coaching—dictated that everybody got a chance to play.

So, at last, the inevitable moment came, and I got waved into the game. But a secret strategic plan, known only to me, soon hatched. I had to walk a tightrope, carefully balancing two diametrically opposing ideas, to survive this accursed gym class with my honor intact. My plan, boiled to its essence, could be summarized as follows:

Get close enough to the action to make it look like I'm willing to get involved, but simultaneously remain far enough away that actually passing the ball to me would be just insane and completely out of the question.

Miraculously, the plan held together for most of my time on the floor. Notice I said most of my time.

The other team's guys had taken the ball down the court and were about to shoot. I ran aimlessly around the general perimeter of the action, staying as close to midcourt as possible. Assuming the other team had taken a shot and made it, I started running full tilt to the other end of the court. And that's when it happened.

Huffing my way down the sideline, trying to gauge where I could continue my involved-yet-avoiding-play master plan, I heard my classmates—including the girls, watching from the rickety old bleachers in that ancient gym—shouting my name over and over.

"Tim!" Hey, I must be really making an impression here …

"Tim!!" Wow, this strategy has everybody fooled …

"Tim, turn around!!!" What? Turn around? Why?

I had assumed incorrectly. The other team never did get off a shot. Somebody on my team stole the ball, saw me running, all alone, toward our basket, and launched the ball the length of the court from the far baseline—and I mean a rocket throw, and right on the money.

"The money," of course, being my face, as I turned around and saw the spinning orange sphere—Wilson ... Wilson ... Wilson— about six inches from my nose, coming in hot, like a lunar module violently re-entering the atmosphere.

It hit me square on the kisser, my glasses sent flying, the rest of me bouncing and somersaulting down the court, legs and arms akimbo, like Evel Knievel hitting the ramp after a motorcycle jump gone desperately awry.

No one ever told us why, but gym class suddenly got canceled. My theory? Simple economics. Father, up at the rectory, didn't need any liability lawsuits emanating from an experimental sixth-grade gym class. Sorry, JFK. Smart guy, that Father. He knew his limitations, too.

Long Division

This story has been dramatized and adapted from actual events. It is shared here to show how some attitudes from a half-century ago have changed but that we still have a lot more work to do.

An otherwise typical Friday morning. *House Party* with Art Linkletter flickered on the television as she ran the sweeper through the modest home. Marjorie, a young mother of Italian heritage, couldn't seem to shake a nagging, gnawing sense of something amiss, though.

Her oldest child, Jimmy, had left that morning for his walk to elementary school with his friends, just as he had every other school day that academic year. The parochial school he attended stood next to the parish church, built at the highest point of their little borough, at the very top of Ormsby Avenue.

"Oh, what's the matter with me?" Marjorie said to herself as she watched her other child, a three-year-old daughter, play with blocks on the living room floor. "I'm getting myself all worked up over nothing. My imagination is running away with me. Everything's fine. We're fine. Our neighborhood's safe. There's no trouble here, and there won't be."

She decided to phone her mother, who lived three blocks away. Just to chat and calm herself down. It had been five years, after all.

Inside an apartment, deep within a complex of multiple buildings, another young mother paced the floor, equally uneasy. But Stacy, an African-American woman, had a very clear idea why.

She had sent her son, Joseph, off to school that morning, as well. A public school, located at the base of Ormsby Avenue. But she had later thought better of it. There'd been a lot of noise in the building the night before, the noise of tension about to snap. Hard, jangling tension. The kind that makes the air itself vibrate.

With the morning's light, some of that dissonance dissipated but not entirely. Their cluster of apartment buildings felt like dry tinder. A single spark could set off a conflagration of race-related rage and riot sure to engulf their world.

And if a fireball loomed for her family—even one that had some elemental justification, considering what had happened the day before—she wanted her boy safe with her, headed somewhere apart from any burgeoning chaos. Stacy decided to contact the school, to pull her son out of there for the day.

———◆———

Inside Sister Clarice's fourth-grade homeroom, Jimmy's class remained chest-deep in a seemingly unending sea of arithmetic problems. Long division, the hardest one of all. Carrying things from one column to the next, realigning the digits into new configurations of numbers as you go. It never felt natural; it never got any easier. But the result always made sense, you had to admit. Getting there was the hard part.

One floor down, in the principal's office, Sister Francis held the receiver. Listening through the veil and wimple on her head, she nodded somberly.

"Yes, Captain, we are aware," she said. "We plan to keep the students inside all day today. Please keep us informed. Yes, thank you. Good-bye."

"Anything you would like me to mimeo for the faculty, Sister?" asked the school secretary.

"Not now, no, Mrs. Griffin," the principal replied, observing out her window onto Ormsby Avenue. "Not yet."

In Room 207, the struggle of Jimmy and his classmates to conquer long division continued.

———————

It took a good twenty-five minutes to walk from her apartment to the public school, so off Stacy went. The phone call to the school never got answered, a potentially bad sign, which only served to stiffen her resolve to extract her son from his sixth-grade classroom, come hell, high water, or unresponsive principals.

"Lord, help this world," she muttered to herself, heels clicking on the cracked and uneven sidewalks, her spring coat ruffling in the wake of her speedy, crisp pace. "But if He won't, I will. Help my family, anyway, small though it might be, just the two of us."

It had been five years since Dallas. Nobody thought it would happen again. Until it did. And now everybody had to figure out where he or she stood. All over again. Damn.

She trotted over the crest of Ormsby Avenue, past the parochial school, and headed down the long, steep hill. Another seven blocks to safety for her and Joseph.

———————

"So, what are you doing, Ma?" Marjorie asked her mother after the elderly woman picked up the phone.

"Oh, nothing. Just put a loaf of bread in the oven. You wanna come down later and bring the little one for a slice of homemade jelly bread?"

"I don't know, Ma. Maybe. I'm feeling a little weird today, like something bad's gonna happen. I don't know. Maybe I'm watching too much TV at night or something."

"Nothing's gonna happen, Margie. Those other places are having all the commotion, not around here. The news never happens here.

Why don't you come on down and have a nice cup of coffee? I want to see the baby."

"Ma, she's four; she's not a baby anymore. I'll see about coming down later. I'll feel better after Jimmy comes home for lunch, okay? Bye, Ma."

As she placed the receiver back onto the wall-mounted rotary kitchen phone, her anxiety didn't get quelled. Quite the opposite. Marjorie felt more nervous than before, as though her adrenal glands had opened the floodgates.

———— ◆ ————

The gaggle of boys in the back of the eighth-grade classroom made no pretense of paying attention to anything the teacher said. The mood started ugly and got worse from there. These kids were hell-bent on making a statement. A grown-up statement. A statement that could not, and would not, be denied, delayed, or deterred.

"After what happened yesterday, we have to stand up and take what's ours," one ringleader said.

"My brother said they're going to wreck the high school today," another contributed. "So, what are we gonna do?"

"We're gonna ditch school at the next class bell, walk up the hill, and beat the shit out of those little Catholic kids up there, that's what. They kill one of ours; we push back where we live. Who's coming with me?"

And with startling speed, the plan to march up to the hilltop school to protest, frighten, and take out some aggression picked up steam among students in the upper grades.

But while these budding demonstrators had not been listening to their teacher, he had indeed been hearing them.

———— ◆ ————

Hot, perspiring, and flushed, Stacy marched into the public school's front doors and straight to the principal's office, just as a male teacher came out of the office, jogging past her, looking concerned.

"Good morning, Mrs. Harris. How may I help you?" asked the secretary.

"I would like to pick up my son and take him out of school today."

"Well, that's a bit unusual. May I ask why?"

"You may ask anything you like, but that doesn't change the fact that I want to pull Joseph out of school for the remainder of the day."

"I'm afraid you'll have to talk with the principal about that, but she is a bit occupied right now on a phone call," said the secretary, a thin veneer of contempt being poorly disguised. "Would you please take a seat?"

Rather than cause a scene, the increasingly aggrieved mother sat down, steaming. About ten minutes later, the secretary went into the principal's office. Fully expecting a confrontation, Stacy girded herself to state and defend her demand once the principal emerged.

Instead, the secretary came back out and said, "We have notified Joseph's teacher. He'll be down here in five minutes, and you can take him for the day. As quickly as possible, actually."

Wow, that sure turned around fast, Stacy thought to herself.

"Miss Lewis, could you get the police on the line for me, please?" came a voice from the principal's office.

———◆———

Sister Francis kept watch out her office window as something unusual appeared to be coalescing at the bottom of Ormsby Avenue, down by the public school. Just then, her phone rang.

"Sister Francis speaking. Yes, Captain, I'm noticing that myself. Thank you, but I believe we will be able to handle this ourselves. I appreciate the call. Yes, good-bye."

She stuck her head out her doorway and ordered Mrs. Griffin to turn on the public-address system. Picking up the microphone, her voice came crackling into every classroom, saying, "Attention, boys and girls. This is Sister Francis speaking. We have decided to dismiss all students early today. We are contacting your parents with instructions that they are to come to the alley behind the school in their cars to pick you up individually. You will not be released from the building until one of your parents, or someone they have designated to act in their absence, has arrived to pick you up. Please behave yourselves and listen to your teachers until you have been taken home. I would now ask all teachers to lead their classes in prayers. Classes will resume as usual on Monday unless your parents have been notified otherwise over the weekend. Thank you."

When the kitchen phone rang, Marjorie knew her intuition was about to be proved right. She listened to the message, hung up the phone, picked up the receiver again, and dialed.

"Ma? I'm bringing the baby down to your place. Something's happening at Jimmy's school."

—◆—

Joseph and his mother left the public school with the intention of catching a trolley to the bus station Downtown, where they could buy tickets to her sister's house in Erie. Things promised to stay calmer there than they were here. They began walking back up Ormsby Avenue to the trolley stop at the intersection with Janius Street, about halfway up the hill.

About thirty seconds later, a swarm of students burst from the same school building, shouting and shaking their fists, as they also started the climb up the hill to the parochial school.

A squad car left the police station, about a quarter mile away, hoping to block the mini mob's progress and steer everyone back into the school.

Marjorie climbed into her car, dropped off her daughter at her mother's house, and started driving to the parochial school to pick up her son.

But unbeknownst to any of these people, word had been spread from bystanders using nearby pay phones that an opportunity for angry, frustrated, simmering adult dissidents to hijack this kiddie protest now existed—and they did just that, in numbers that surprised everyone.

For this was not just any Friday morning. This was Friday, April 5, 1968, the morning after the assassination of the Rev. Martin Luther King Jr., and the nation had begun to explode in anger and righteous indignation. While other cities saw riots and destruction, this little borough had been spared. But that was about to change.

A couple of windows on parked cars got smashed as the crowd made its way up Ormsby. Many of the students got scared, realizing they had started something in youthful bravado that quickly careened out of their control into something truly dangerous. They started running in all directions, some back to the school building, others toward their homes, some just running anywhere to get away from the growing violence that the adults around them started considering or committing.

Marjorie pulled the Rambler into the alley behind the school, and Jimmy quickly ran to the car. They came around the corner onto Ormsby and saw a crowd heading their way, taking up the whole width of the street. If she could make it to Janius Street before the demonstrators got there, they could take a different route and make it home safely.

Stacy and Joseph stood at the trolley stop watching the mob get closer. The trolleys ran every seven minutes, and they'd been standing there more than eight. Where was that trolley? As a car came past them, a driver rolled down his window and said, "Hey, the buses and trolleys stopped running today because of the protests and problems that are starting up around town. There ain't no trolley coming for you and your kid, Ma'am. Sorry."

Just then, some of the adult demonstrators coming up the hill shouted, "Hey, lady! You with us? They killed Dr. King, and you and your boy ain't gonna do nothin' about it? You're just like us. Don't run away. You need to be with us, or there's gonna be trouble for you."

Marjorie drove to the corner, with the crowd still about a half block away. "Make sure your doors are locked, Jimmy," she said, noticing a woman and young boy frantically looking about, a panicked expression on their faces.

Within seconds, Stacy ran to the Rambler, slapped her hands on the driver's window, and shouted, "Can you please get us away from all this? I just want to get my son to a safe place!"

"Mom, that's Joseph. He plays Pee-Wee football with me. I know him; he's nice," said the young voice beside Marjorie on the passenger seat.

The squad car came tearing down Janius, blocking the intersection with Ormsby, just as Joseph and his mother climbed into the Rambler. Marjorie hit the gas and took a hard left onto Janius, speeding away from the bubbling mayhem.

Once the police arrived, the mob dissolved in minutes, and any students still in the area returned to the public school. Other than the guy with the crowbar who got hauled in for the car window smashings, no other arrests were made. And students at the parochial school got a jump on their weekend—although most never understood the circumstances that led to it.

The borough remained safe for another day, but most residents remained blissfully unaware how close the situation had come to spinning out of control.

At Jimmy's grandma's house, the two boys, their mothers, and his little sister sat around the kitchen table, the grown-ups sipping coffee and the kids enjoying some homemade jelly spread on freshly baked bread. The bus ride to Erie would not be necessary.

A "long-division" problem—people divided from each other for a long time, unnecessarily—got solved. At least with one small group of mothers and sons. And at least for one day.

Long division, the hardest kind of problem. Carrying ideas from one place to the next, realigning attitudes and assumptions into new configurations as you go. It might not always feel natural; it might not get any easier. But the result always makes sense, you have to admit.

Getting there is the hard part.

Big Little Books for President

In the prehistoric days before FM or satellite radio in the car, much less iPods or Twitter or any of the myriad media options to occupy one's attention these days, we had something different. Something old fashioned. Something better.

We had Big Little Books.

Many a car ride to a favorite aunt's house, to church on Sunday morning, or to some event or another, was spent in the back seat of our family's brown Chevelle with my two sisters. Rather than snipe with either (or both) of them, I'd settle in with a Big Little Book. A quiet, peaceful backseat full of kids made Mom happy, too.

Big Little Books were a wonderful invention by Whitman Publishing Co. back in the 1930s. They featured full-length stories, including some of the classics but mostly pulpy comic-book characters or superhero tales. The great feature, though, was that each book fit in the palm of your hand, measuring about four and a half inches high by three and a half inches across, and that a full-page illustration faced every page of text.

I can remember reading Aquaman and Fantastic Four stories, along with Tom Sawyer, the Lone Ranger, and some other favorites. When you enjoyed a story in a Big Little Book, you forgot you were reading. The pages flew by, and the steady stream of illustrations helped move the story along swiftly, as well.

Big Little Books opened the doorway to the concept of reading for enjoyment for millions of kids, myself included. They probably helped formulate the idea in my head, from the earliest years of elementary school, that I wanted to be a writer. An appreciation of words and how they can move an idea forward has appealed to me my whole life, and those compact storybooks might have lit that particular fuse.

Keeping things simple, easy to follow, and even enjoyable when you can. That's the essence of good writing that persuades and encourages people to act.

Conversely, with around ten weeks before the big election in November, the level of nonsense and diversions and distractions and distortions and mischaracterizations and pomposity and denials and accusations—you know what I mean—is guaranteed to reach epic proportions. And that's so sick, so unworthy, so disrespectful to the electorate.

Wouldn't it be nice, would it be too much to ask, could we possibly hope, that our candidates—from the local school board to Congress to the White House—follow the wonderful example of the Big Little Books?

State your case simply, clearly, and honestly. Be respectful, both of your opponent and of the office to which you aspire. Make your argument easy to follow. Show us that you understand the vision, concerns, and fears of your potential constituents and that you have a plan to address them. Let us get to know you as a person, not just as a slogan or a vague promise.

Honor us with your effort. Have enough faith to level with us. Trust us enough to provide a story about yourself that fits in the palm of our hands. There's too much riding on this election for anything less.

I never finished a Big Little Book and felt cheated or angry or disappointed or as though I needed to take a shower from all the nastiness. It would be great to feel that same way after a hard-fought campaign, regardless of who wins in the end.

Good Morning, Sister Frederick!

S ister Frederick knew how to run a Catholic school.
   She never raised her voice in the eight years we both inhabited
   St. Joseph School, she as the principal, I as an elementary school
pupil. Way back when, Catholic schools sported a nun-to-lay-teacher
ratio of about 50-to-50, and my experience bore that out, with four
sisters and four missuses.

But no matter whether your teacher had joined a religious order
or not, Sister Frederick was always at the helm, steering our little but
proud inner-city school through the shoals of late-1960s, early-1970s
social chaos, upheaval, and mayhem.

You would be quietly listening to instructions on an arithmetic problem, or intently completing exercises in your Think-and-Do
book, or wondering whether the little store on the next block had in
stock any more Pee-Chee folders (because you had colored in all of
the drawings of people playing sports) or those plastic pencils with
ten lead refill inserts (right inside the pencil!) when the door to the
classroom would open and in strode Sister Frederick. And you knew
what to do, if you knew what was good for you.

The class, en masse, including the teacher, would immediately stand up and announce with vigor, "Good morning, Sister
Frederick!" To which she would reply, "Good morning, class. How
are you today?" Which led us to the unchanging and unchangeable

rejoinder, "Fine, thank you. How are *you* today?" "I am fine. Please be seated." "Thank you, Sister Frederick!" And we'd all sit down in unison. No stragglers allowed, no freelancing or ad-libbing on the dialogue, either, Buster.

Anyone who tried any funny stuff—and got caught—knew what was coming next. We called it the Peppermint Stick. Sister Frederick never used it much, but, again, she didn't need to. Once you heard some wiseacre getting his just deserts out in the hallway, the chilling effect was considerable. Thinking back on it, I'd say Sister Frederick really knew what she was doing. We never actually saw the punishment being applied (Whack!); we just heard it, which created a much stronger impression and made it even more effective in preventing future high jinks.

After eight years at St. Joe's, we moved on to high school, and for most of my friends and me, that meant switching to a public high school. Quite a culture change, but a good one in a lot of ways.

I can remember one Saturday night when a couple of my buddies and I walked up to church to attend Mass before hanging out the rest of the evening. For whatever reason—probably because we got there at the last possible second—the church was really crowded, and the only open pew was way in front, directly behind Sister Frederick and couple of other nuns.

Assuming diplomatic immunity—we had not been under her jurisdiction for the past two years, after all—we weren't worried about her yelling at us in church as my friends and I kept up our teenaged dialogue going through most of the service.

We finally came to the sign of peace, where everyone extends a hand to others generally within reach to wish them blessings. So I shook hands with my buddies and the people on either side of us. Then Sister Frederick turned around. She had a smile on her face, but her eyes were not exactly wishing us peace. In an instant, I was eleven again, hoping to not get the Peppermint Stick.

"Peace be with you," she said through gritted teeth, shaking each of our hands and still smiling. "And if I hear one more word from you three, you will join me after Mass for a little talk."

"Yes, Sister Frederick," we all responded in unison. And that was the last thing any of us said until we walked out of that church that evening.

You know, despite her insistence on running a tight ship, we also knew that Sister Frederick had a heart. She cared about us kids, even long after we had left her direct charge. She cared enough to make sure that we knew our manners, that respecting the people in charge made sense and gave order, and that when you got out of line, something had to be done to correct that behavior.

I think our American society would be in much better shape today if there were more Sister Fredericks around.

Rocket Ship to the North Pole

W e've crashed through the chronological wall into December now, so it's a no-holds-barred, downhill-with-no-brakes sprint to the Big One—the holiday that bespectacled Red Ryder BB Gun-lusting Ralphie Parker described as "lovely, glorious, beautiful Christmas, around which the entire kid year revolved" in the movie *A Christmas Story*.

Like Ralphie, Christmas brought a series of recurring events and themes when I was a kid.

Take Paul Shannon on Channel 4's *Adventure Time* after-school TV show, for instance. For eleven months out of the year, he would play old *Beetle Bailey* and *Kimba the White Lion* cartoons, show Three Stooges shorts, and host a Cub Scout or Brownie troop in the little on-set bleachers. The kids would sing mossy old standards such as "Bingo Was His Name-O" or "A Great Big Brownie Smile" or "If You're Happy and You Know It." Predictable, comforting, regular. You knew what you were getting, plopping yourself down in front of the TV after a tough day among the nuns, with *Adventure Time*.

But starting right around December 1, crafty old Paul Shannon would bring out his annual showstopper: the Rocket Ship to the North Pole.

This opened the floodgates to every kid in Pittsburgh to write letters to Santa, making their wish lists for presents. You would mail them in to Channel 4, and every day Paul Shannon would take a fistful of these hand-scrawled pleas for wagons, dolls, and probably a BB gun or two and read some out loud while tossing them into a special door on the side of the rocket.

After about ten minutes of this—as you stared, bug-eyed, at home, waiting to get confirmation that your letter would make it on that day's delivery run—Paul Shannon would close the hatch, start the Mission Control countdown, and the Rocket Ship to the North Pole would be seen blasting off from its launch pad into the sky. How awesome was that? To know that you and your buddies, sitting in your living rooms in Pittsburgh, Pennsylvania, had an advocate with an express rocket route to Santa Claus!

When I was little, I bought the whole bit. Paul Shannon had a Rocket Ship to the North Pole, doggone it, and I had to get my letter to Channel 4 at all costs. And you can bet I did, year after year. Even heard my name on TV once, so I knew my letter was on its jet-propulsed way to Santa that afternoon.

Yeah, awesome and comforting at the same time. No wonder *Adventure Time* killed in the ratings during its time slot back then.

Eventually you get older and the scales fall from your eyes. I had the opportunity to actually be in the bleachers during the live broadcast of *Adventure Time* one day and got an eyeful. The bright colors on the set surrounding the bleachers were for the cameras and the kids watching at home, I learned. The back of those set pieces, though—the ones that you saw while sitting on those bleachers—were of old soda pop boxes and plywood. My first peek into the hidden, disappointing, disheartening underbelly of show business, I suppose.

Paul Shannon was very nice to us kids that day, but he was with us only during the segments when we were on the air. I got so flustered I forgot how to spell B-I-N-G-O when our big moment arrived.

But most of all, I thank Providence to this day that I wasn't in-studio during the run-up to Christmas. I'm a grown man now, and I know that there's not really a Rocket Ship to the North Pole that launched from Paul Shannon's studio at Channel 4 every weekday in

December at 4:45 p.m. I know that the "rocket" he stood beside was a plywood shell with a little door for the letters. I know that the sight of the thing blasting into the air was actually a clip they used and reused from an actual NASA launch.

But I didn't know all of those things back then. And I'm so glad I didn't. Christmas for kids is about believing in the unbelievable. That's what makes it so awesome. And so comforting.

The Busyness of Business

Sitting at my old wood-and-wrought iron desk, the smell of floor wax and fresh pencil shavings wafting through the antique, musty, dusty classroom, I stared at the list of words that Mr. H. was screaming at us to finish working on.

We were converting nouns from a description into a personal state, as in "happy" to "happiness," or "hopeful" to "hopefulness." It was either English or spelling class. It's all a blur, for the most part.

But one part of the lesson that has remained very clear in my mind surrounded the word "busy."

Mr. H. called on me to give the answer, naturally, and I suddenly became torn. Was the converted word "busyness" or "business?" I decided the correct response was "business." Mr. H. did not agree. His teacher's guide read "busyness," and that was that.

Actually, for giving the "wrong" answer, I got off pretty light. Mr. H. used to whip chalkboard erasers, pencils, even his car keys at the heads of kids who dozed off or gave stupid answers in class. These were the golden days of parochial education, after all, when discipline meant whatever the teacher said it meant.

Anyway, the difference between "busyness" and "business" still intrigues me. After two decades spent within large organizations, I saw way too many people who believed – and behaved – as though the two were synonymous. As if "being busy" were the same as "conducting business."

And they're not.

An uncle who had served in the Army long ago told me once that, to stay out of trouble and avoid unnecessary or unpalatable assignments, a private's best friend was a clipboard. Just walk around, looking like you're doing something important, jotting stuff down on that clipboard, and they'll usually leave you alone, he said. That's busyness, not business.

As a standalone consultant, I've absolutely no time for busyness. When you need to find the work, perform the work, invoice the work, and receive payment for the work yourself, every minute counts. It's got to be all business, when the alternative means you and your family go homeless and hungry.

According to the U.S. Department of Labor's Bureau of Labor Statistics, nonfarm business sector labor productivity decreased at a 2.0 percent annual rate, reflecting increases of 0.1 percent in output and 2.2 percent in hours worked. In other words, it took people longer to produce something during the most recent quarter, nationwide.

Can this be attributed to a disproportionate amount of "busyness" compared with focused, concentrated, applied effort in conducting meaningful "business?" It's hard to say with any certainty, but my guess is that some of that comes into play.

Sure, everybody needs to blow off steam and little slice of time occasionally. When merely looking busy with your little Army clipboard gets a pass. But when "busyness" supersedes real "business"— where products get produced efficiently and sold for a profit, which enables companies to improve facilities, hire more people, and increase salaries—that's where the trouble starts.

And it doesn't take having a teacher throw his car keys at your head for that basic business truism to sink in.

Taking One for the Team

We all know one. The dad who misses the first inning of a big game to park the car and walk to the field from a distance. The lineman who sacrifices his body to protect the quarterback so that the team can score. The mother who spends that Wednesday shopping and cleaning, then cooks a turkey and a bounteous meal that special November Thursday, while everyone else snacks and talks and watches parades and football.

These people rarely get the credit they deserve and have earned, but they're not looking for credit. They're not looking for glory or fishing for compliments. They're the great unsung heroes, and they carry out their heroism humbly.

I was an unsung hero once. But I demanded some credit. I longed for glory and compliments. I was not humble. I was mad, and wanted restitution for my sacrifice. Here's how it went down.

Age nine, Cub Scout den meets at my house, Mom serves as Den Mother, the big Halloween Pack Meeting looming and our little den wants to blow those other dens' doors off with something spectacular, unrivaled in the annals of Scouting.

Before long, eureka! We will recreate the (then brand-new) Peanuts story of the Great Pumpkin! And not as ourselves as recognizable Cub Scouts, but with actual 3-D recreations of Charlie Brown and everyone in the TV special. Hah! Take *that*, you sorry other dens. Prepare for epicness at the local Moose Hall in three weeks.

We actually had a spitting chance to win first place in this talent competition, unlike my cursed luck with the Pinewood Derby races, where no matter how fast my little "Yellow Lightning" car zoomed around my bedroom, when it had to perform in front of more than two people it forgot how to run in a straight line. But this Peanuts thing felt like a stroke of genius. A sure thing. A slam dunk before anybody knew what a slam dunk was.

Mom performed above and beyond with this project. She took the leap and led ten little male doofuses into the tricky, sticky quicksand of papier-mâché. Bless her heart, she's the most courageous woman I know.

If memory serves, we started by blowing up some really big balloons, then dunked long, wide strips of newspaper into the goop and draped them over, around, and under those balloons, ending up with pretty good "heads" for the characters. A week later at the next den meeting, the papier-mâché had dried, so we popped the balloons and started paining on faces, poking holes so we could see out, and making an opening big enough to get the things over our noggins. All the main Peanuts characters had a part—Charlie Brown, Linus, Snoopy, Pig Pen, the Great Pumpkin himself, and…*Lucy*.

LUCY?!

Hold the phone here, Mom. This is a gaggle of Cub Scouts. We can't have a Lucy! We are of one mind on this point, right guys?

Well, we not only ended up with a Lucy—who was pretty integral to the story—but guess who got to play the role? Yep, yours truly. Taking one for the team. The unsung hero, that's me.

Some are born to perform in drag, others have it thrust upon them. But I did not go quietly into that papier-mâché performance. I had some clauses built into my contract to protect myself from the avalanche of Monday morning abuse this Friday night fiasco would surely produce in class, should word get around who was inside that big round female head.

My terms. <u>One</u>: I would absolutely *not* wear a dress.

<u>Two</u>: No dialogue for Lucy. She would work in mime for the first time ever.

<u>Three</u>: The whole troupe would enter the Moose Hall's big meeting room together in full giant-head regalia and nondescript sheets, and leave the same way. We would accept our applause once we had returned, completely out of costume.

<u>Four</u>: Everyone in the den would swear to keep his big trap shut about this forevermore. These conditions were accepted, and the show went ahead as planned.

Fact is, we killed at the Pack Meeting. No one saw it coming. We won the competition, hands down. We blew their doors off. A theatrical triumph in every way.

I had it made in the shade Monday morning as our class settled in for the day. Or so I thought. Just before the morning prayer and Pledge of Allegiance, the kid behind me leaned over and whispered in my ear, "Nice wig...*Lucy*."

So much for Scouts honor.

CARRICK HIGH, CARRICK HIGH:
Forever We'll Be True

Wading into a sea of twenty-four hundred students, after having come from the tiny bubble of a student body at St. Joe's, took some getting used to. First you looked for the kids you grew up with, and then the circle widened to other kids who came from Catholic grade schools. And by sophomore year, none of that mattered; you all came from Carrick High. From the school newspaper to the marching band, from advanced academic classes to trying to become invisible in gym class, high school remains four of the most impactful, crazy, fantastic years of my life.

'Feelin's'

High school carries countless inferences for people. For many, it represented a time of testing and teasing and tears. For others, it brought brimming waves of temporary glory, all but guaranteed to fade in subsequent years.

High school for me still shines as four years of great friends, great times, and pretty good grades. Music provided the thread that ran through those years, underscoring and underpinning just about everything that made high school such a treasured stitch in time.

One of the most enjoyable musical escapades back then came via a four-piece band I played in called Limit. Don't ask me what that name means. We picked it from a speed-limit sign outside the lead guitarist's house one night after practice. Hey, I said we played in a band; nobody said anything about being deep thinkers.

Anyway, Limit comprised a guy on lead guitar, another guy on keyboards, a girl on rhythm guitar, and me on drums and lead vocals. No, that is not a typo. And yes, you may stop laughing now.

We practiced once or twice a week in the lead guitarist's basement, playing Top 40 tunes for the most part, and we actually were pretty good. We played wedding receptions every weekend from May to September, picking up between $100 and $150 per band member per gig. Not bad dough for a bunch of high school kids during the "malaise" years under Jimmy Carter.

While my friends flipped burgers and swept floors for minimum wage, I got to sing and play drums with my friends for some serious cash. Deep thinkers? Maybe not. But budding capitalists? You bet.

The only hitch in this adolescent adventure came by way of our rhythm guitarist's father. A very nice man, who drove his daughter to practice and to gigs. But unlike the rest of the parents who got us to our performances, this fellow never left. I would like to think that happened because he wanted to protect his daughter, and I'm sure that played a part.

But the primary reason he always hung around, I fear, was that he wanted to sing in a band.

He always struck me as a Vegas lounge crooner who, to his everlasting dismay, never quite landed that big break. How he thought that latching onto a bunch of city-punk high school kids playing wedding receptions and Friday night gigs in local bars was going to improve his odds, I never could figure out.

As Limit got some traction and we lined up some regular dates, this fellow's hints about singing at least one song with us grew more insistent, until the lead guitarist finally relented. We gave him the one song that none of us wanted: "Feelings," a four-minute puddle of slush sung by some cat named Morris Albert that inexplicably clung onto the charts in the mid-'70s for way too long. But it was too popular not to have in our set, so this gave us the perfect out.

The only problem came in that our guest vocalist loved that song. Looooved it. Adored it. Wanted to take it out behind the bleachers and make out with it. And, as such, performed the ever-loving hell out of it. At least from his perspective, anyway.

The vocal stylings included some peculiar pronunciations, as in "Feeeeee-lin's," an overly chummy and casual treatment—certainly not the Morris Albert-approved enunciation, "Feeeeee-lings." Cringeworthy, trust me. We tried to time the song for when the greatest number of people had headed to the restrooms. But as insufferable as it sounded, we needed his daughter's rhythm guitar, so he got his shot once each gig. Don't think he ever made it to Vegas, though. Not as a singer, that's for sure.

Maybe we turned out to be deeper thinkers than we realized.

A Near-Grape Incident

The music folder for my high school band weighed a ton. I didn't want to lug it around school with me all day, and my locker couldn't have been any farther from the band room, so I kept it in what I thought was a safe cupboard near the drum section.

So imagine my shock and horror when, one fine spring morning during my senior year, I reached into my terrific hiding place to find no folder. No anything. No marching band music, no concert band music, no jazz band music. All gone.

I tore up the entire band room, all of the small practice rooms, the closets where the marching band uniforms hung in storage. Bupkus. Nothing. The well kept coming up dry. My folder had disappeared. What to do?

In the stupendously lacking brain of a seventeen-year-old, the strategy immediately came into focus. Fake it. Stall. Delay. Deny. Try to play my parts by memory. Dodge. Do anything but admit that all of my music had been misplaced by my own carelessness and laziness, probably forever. Who'd know or notice, anyway?

You can guess how well that brilliant strategy worked—especially on those musical pieces where it was my job to bang away on the timpani, those big, booming brass kettledrums. I'm there, cowering in the back corner of the orchestra, going purely on guts and guesses.

And when you guess wrong on the timpani, pal, everybody knows it. Everybody. It isn't like the sixth flute player down the line hitting a wrong note. No, no, no. When you bring that mallet down—Boom! Rrrrrrummmmmmbbbblllllllll—all seventy-five other kids in the room can tell when you've come in too early, too late, too fast, too slow. Which was too bad for me.

I shanked one on the kettledrum just like that a day or two after the realization that I would be music-less for the remainder of my high school career. Mr. B., the band director, snapped his head up faster than grease off a hot frying pan, his eyes boring a hole in my forehead.

"Hayes, what the hell are you playing back there?" he shouted after stopping the ensemble. My friends in the drum section could see there was nothing on my music stand, but the director couldn't.

"Sorry," I said, hoping he'd forget it and start everybody up again. Naturally, he didn't.

"When are you supposed to come in after letter *C*?" he asked me. "Can you tell?"

"Yep, I got it."

"I hope so. All right, let's take it from letter *C*."

Panic had seized hold of my head, my hands, my heart. I suddenly got blanketed in fibrillation and fluster. I had no idea when to come in after letter *C*. How could I? This lowbrow, half-assed fakery continued for the remainder of the period, and I knew the jig was up. As the bell rang for the next class, Mr. B. gestured for me to follow him to his desk.

"Where's your music?" he asked, of course sussing out the issue out on his own.

Any hope of my becoming a master criminal, outsleuthing the Sherlock Holmeses of the world, pretty much went out the window at that moment.

"I don't know. I lost it. I had put it in a cupboard over there, and a couple of days ago it was gone."

He looked at me, this man for whom I had so much respect through four years of high school. The thought that I'd let him down? Absolutely crushing. Unthinkable. Unbearable.

"Keep looking, Hayes," he said. "It'll turn up. We only have one timpani player, and that's you. Who else would want your music? Don't turn into a grape."

In Mr. B.'s vernacular, a *grape* was someone who didn't pull his or her weight for the band and the other student musicians. Like wearing the Cone of Shame. No one ever wanted to be labeled a grape.

"Okay, Mr. B."

You know, the crazy thing is that folder did turn up two days later, in the same place I'd put it before all this happened. I never found out who took it in the first place, or why they decided to put it back—I have a pretty good idea, but never could confirm it—but I'm glad they did.

Huge life lesson learned during this particular adolescent adventure: Tell the truth, right up front. That's the only way a problem can get solved. Take your medicine, and keep moving forward. People forgive when they know the truth and can help you make things right again.

After all, Bill Clinton wasn't impeached because of his peccadilloes—but because he lied and covered them up. Martha Stewart didn't go to jail because of insider trading—but because she lied and covered it up. The truth really does come out in the end. But it hurts a lot less if it comes out in the beginning.

On the night of graduation, as the band played various selections during the ceremony, after I got my diploma and walked back to the band, I came up to Mr. B. to shake his hand one last time, and to say good-bye and thanks, when he said to me, "Congratulations, Hayes. You were almost a grape there for a minute, but you pulled through. You've done a great job, and I'm proud of you. Don't forget about us."

As a result, I left high school five feet off the ground. Grape-less, wiser, and blessed.

A Leap of Faith

Whistling through my local Target the other day, it immediately became obvious that the start of a new school year—for college students in particular—loomed, and loomed large.

It also became obvious that, with my kids at least, we had made it past those days of racking up hundreds of dollars worth of desk lamps, end tables, picture frames, new clothes, shoes, laptops, and other collegiate supplies, at long last.

Then, on my drive back home, I tuned into the oldies station here and landed smack in the middle of a replay of an old *American Top 40* program with Casey Kasem, from the week ending August 8, 1978—mere days before I left for college for the first time. I listened to the rest of that program, from Number 23 ("Running Away" by Jefferson Starship) to Number 1 ("Miss You" by the Rolling Stones), and found myself back with long hair, short gym shorts, huge aviator eyeglasses, and a sense of excitement, impatience, and coursing adrenaline, champing at the bit to dive into this amazing new chapter of life.

Remember in *Indiana Jones and the Last Crusade* when Indy heads into the bowels of the cave to find the Holy Grail? One of the challenges, created by an optical illusion, gives the impression that he is about to step out into nothing but a sheer, fatal fall into a stone gorge.

Before Indy realizes that a perfectly safe path does indeed stretch to the other side, he closes his eyes, extends his leg, and tells himself, "It's a leap of faith," before his foot finds solid ground and he continues on the trek.

That's the sensation I dealt with that late summer of 1978. My job that sweltering season entailed painting gigantic garage doors, with about twenty small windows each, at a truck terminal. Between the smell of the oil-based paint, the dirt and grit from tractor-trailer exhaust, the nasty emissions from a chemical plant across the road, and the punishingly humid ninety-plus-degree heat that summer, the notion of heading off to a cool, leafy, shady autumn college campus in pursuit of pure knowledge sounded like heaven on earth.

I had a great many good friends in high school and had a wonderful four years there. At the same time, the notion of starting fresh, among a much larger pool of students from other states and other parts of the world, in an environment that encouraged not only studies but learning how to live—your own life, certainly, and in peace and cooperation with others—really lit my fire.

A dear cousin who had attended the same university a couple of years ahead of me once said that your high school friends might be great, but the friends you make in college are the ones you keep for life, a statement that has proved to be absolutely true. Most of those high school friends, so treasured while we attended school together as teenagers, remained a part of my circle for a few months once college began, but then we eventually lost touch—only to reunite about a year ago at a funeral home after one of them passed away very unexpectedly. It had been more than thirty-five years—enough for two full high school-aged lives to have passed—since we'd all been in the same room together.

My family somehow put up with me that summer before leaving for college—an amazing statement because I must have been even more insufferable than usual. Two songs, whenever they happened to come on the radio, guaranteed my sending a full-blast-volume beatdown out my bedroom window to the unsuspecting world below.

The first? "Indiana Wants Me" by R. Dean Taylor, which tells the story of an escapee from the Indiana State Penitentiary being tracked down by police. That didn't matter to me, though. I just loved shouting the line "Indiana wants me" because I was headed off to Indiana University of Pennsylvania. The second song had actually climbed the charts that summer of '78, "Movin' Out" by Billy Joel, and became a favorite for obvious reasons.

Certain life moments represent such potential, carry such energy, and hold such promise, they create indelible memories that can be conjured up again with the right provocation, like my stroll through Target and hearing those old songs on the radio. Parents of college-bound children, take special note.

Thinking back on my final days as a "kid," before the transition into college student and adult, certainly qualifies as one of those times for me. Because my life certainly did take an entirely new trajectory once I moved onto campus.

How, you ask?

Well, I met her the second day there. And last month, we marked our thirty-fourth wedding anniversary. I just knew college was gonna be amazing. A leap of faith, indeed, and one that has never stopped paying the greatest dividends imaginable.

The Poop-Out Bus

My daughter just successfully completed her first half marathon last weekend. Obviously she got my long-distance endurance genes. As if. Allow me to explain.

Eons ago, while a freshman in high school, my friends and I signed up to participate in a twenty-mile walk all over the city of Pittsburgh to raise money for some charity—muscular dystrophy or the March of Dimes. Doesn't really matter now.

You asked people to pledge a certain amount for each mile, and on the big day it made for some happy film for the Saturday evening TV news as hundreds of people took a long stroll around the city on behalf of a good cause.

The morning of the event, my buddies and I hopped a bus Downtown to the starting line. We had on our everyday tennis shoes and blue jeans. This would be a piece of cake. Twenty miles? Ha! Child's play. We were a bunch of cocky fourteen-year-old guys. What could possibly stop us?

Off to the side sat a big yellow school bus with a giant banner reading Poop-Out Bus hanging from both sides.

"Ho, the Poop-Out Bus!" we howled. "How big of a wuss would you have to be to get on that thing?"

Before long the whistles sounded and we began the march out to the far neighborhoods and back Downtown. Our little gang hung together for the first five or six miles, talking, laughing, having a good time being young goofballs together. At about mile ten, some of the guys speeded up, wanting to run for a while. I, being strategic about the event all of a sudden, thought it best to conserve energy and just maintain a steady walking pace.

Those stiff blue jeans—more like dungarees, actually—started to chafe, just a little. But, nah, nothing to worry about. We were half-way done already, weren't we? Yeah, piece of cake. It was all downhill from here.

Over the next three miles, I seemed to lose my entire cluster of friends. Alone, thighs chafing so badly I could fry eggs on them and left to wonder why I ever signed up for this Bataan Death March on the Monongahela, I saw the Poop-Out Bus coming up from the rear.

Here was my chance. Flag down that stupid thing, take a seat, have some water, cool off my blazing behind, and get back Downtown before anybody else. They won't be able to figure out how I arrived before them. I could cement my high school reputation right then and there.

It took every bit of willpower, but I resisted the lure of the Poop-Out Bus. On I walked, coming over the crest of a hill and seeing the tops of the Downtown skyscrapers on the horizon. It couldn't have been more than three more miles to the finish line.

But why, in the name of all that is holy, did I wear these accursed blue jeans today of all days? Afraid to look down, for fear of seeing myself engulfed in a raging inferno, I felt my feet and legs scream-ing for relief. In the days before sneakers engineered with more attention than the space shuttle, we had a flat strip of rubber for a sole and a wafer-thin slice of alleged foam for arch support. It was like walking with a mouse pad stuck to the bottom of your feet. For twenty miles.

Hot, tired, sore, fed up, and with nobody I knew in sight to make fun of me later, I succumbed to the inevitable and caught the next

Poop-Out Bus. Had I hit the wall, in the parlance of long-distance runners? No, actually, I think the wall hit me.

Dame Fortune rode with me, though, because just as I disembarked, the majority of my friends made it to the finish line. The bus's drop-off spot stood off to the side, so nobody saw me get off. I craftily snuck into the general flow of walkers and caught up with my buddies, telling them I had been within sight of them for miles.

Because, you know, the Poop-Out Bus? How big of a wuss would you have to be to get on that thing?

Mr. C. and the Called Third Strike

"Life isn't fair," said Mr. C., our high school sophomore English teacher. It was his standard comeback when you received an essay with a grade you didn't like, or when the class would go off on a tangent about the injustice of current events.

Decades later, I've caught myself telling my own kids those very same words, and the memory of Mr. C. comes flashing back into vivid living color. Of course, he was right back then, and he'd still be right today.

But that doesn't mean we have to passively accept the notion that "life isn't fair." All that does – or all that should do – is define the terms of engagement. In the world of leadership communication, that means knowing that there will be opposition to any position you take, so preparation in anticipating and overcoming it evens the odds.

Think of the killer question ahead of time, the one you'd rather not have to answer, and have a credible answer ready anyway. Build into your remarks explanations of as many points of contention as possible, thereby heading off your critics. When you don't know, say so, but promise to get an answer quickly. Strong opposition to what you believe as true, good, and credible may not be fair, but if you're ready to defend it, you've at least evened things out.

Then there are times when the unfairness of life can just go off the rails completely, and a rational response becomes a super-human, Herculean, gargantuan challenge. Like an infamous called third strike at a community league baseball game a few years ago.

I had rushed home from a day of seeing clients to make it to the last half of my son's game. If they won, they'd make it to the play-offs, which is a big deal for a bunch of fifth- and sixth-grade guys. The coach of the other team was one of these boorish, pushy, loud knuckleheads who thinks he's constantly playing the seventh game of the World Series. His son was pitching, and by some fluke of scheduling (yeah, right), his other, older, son was umpiring behind home plate.

As the game progressed, I could see ahead to a scenario where my son could end up at bat with two outs in the final inning, the game on his shoulders. Sometimes I wish I weren't so good at seeing ahead, because that's precisely what happened. We were down by one run with two outs, one runner on base, and my kid walking up to home plate.

He fouled one off, strike one. He took a couple outside, two balls and one strike. He swung and missed, two and two. Next came a brush-back, high and inside, full count.

"Please, God, let this be a hit or a ball, but let him get on base," I whispered from the little set of bleachers off the third-base line. What happened next could have straightened even Mr. C.'s curly blond hair. In the annals of life not being fair, this one goes into the Hall of Fame.

The pitch came in low. So low, in fact, that it hit the dirt in front of home plate. In *front*, mind you. It even kicked up a cloud of dirt into the air, almost to prove the point without a doubt. My kid saw it and didn't swing, naturally. Everybody saw it! How could you possibly miss it? Ball four, right? Batter take your base, right?

"Strike three!" called the ump. And I thought I would jump out of my skin in anger and shock. In full impress-the-client regalia, suit, tie, wing-tip shoes, the whole deal, I shot off of those bleachers, ran up to that punk umpire and shouted things that would make my mother wish she'd never met me. Our team's coaches had to pull me away before there was an all-out bench-clearing brouhaha right there in our idyllic little neighborhood playground.

What did I say before about adults being boorish, pushy, loud knuckleheads? Well, at least our side had one that day, too. I guess that made it—well—fair.

What I Learned Watching *Bowling for Dollars*

I n the 1970s, on Pittsburgh's Channel 4, a thirty-minute cultural touchstone was beamed into homes every evening at seven o'clock. Its name? *Bowling for Dollars.*

Hosted by local legend Nick Perry—who later served time in prison for masterminding the infamous "6-6-6" Pennsylvania Lottery fix—*Bowling for Dollars* gave local yonkos a chance at some fabulous cash prizes based on how many pins they could knock down given two rolls of the ball. Two strikes got you a hundred bucks, if memory serves, and the winnings sank dramatically from those towering heights.

Good old Nick proved a winning host, amiably chatting up the bowlers as they emerged from behind the cardboard-and-plywood set, giving them a chance to calm their nerves before approaching the two-lane, in-studio alley. What a TV station was doing with a two-lane bowling alley inside the building is a mystery that might never be adequately solved, but I digress.

I saw a neighbor or two take a shot on the show, along with a high school classmate once. Yeah, they even let teenagers on. I'm telling you, *Bowling for Dollars* was a happening.

But there was one contestant in particular whose five minutes of fame scorched themselves into my brain so deeply that I can still see it all these years later. Tony. Tony from Munhall.

Nick Perry, handheld microphone at the ready, announces Tony from Munhall, who proudly springs into view. Now remember, this is circa 1976. Tony from Munhall is the walking, talking embodiment of every '70s cliché imaginable. He's got the shades, even though the show obviously occurs indoors. He's got the lime green combination disco/leisure suit with the lapels big enough to rival the back fins of a Cadillac. He's got the polyester shirt with the buttons open enough to show off his chest fuzz and about fifteen gold necklaces. He is oozing, radiating, waves of cool, is Tony from Munhall.

At least in his own head, that is.

Nick, as was his style, asks whether Tony from Munhall would like to say hello to anyone out there in TV land. Tony from Munhall cocks his head, adjusts his shades, lets his slicked-back hair reflect those hot studio lights for a moment, points his finger right into the lens, and says, "You know it, Nicky. I just want to say hi to all you cool cats and kitties out there."

And the great moment arrives. Tony from Munhall strides over to the lanes, white leather shoes and superwide bellbottoms moving smoothly. He nods to the tiny little bleachers where the studio audience watched the proceedings, picks up his bowling ball, lines up his first toss ...

... and promptly throws a gutter ball.

"Not to worry," comes the calming voice of Nick Perry. "You still can make some money with the next ball, Tony."

His icy cool now starting to get a little slushy, Tony from Munhall shakes off the miscue, waits for the ball return, picks up the devilish three-holed sphere again, lines himself up, sends it down the alley ...

... and throws *another* gutter ball.

All of us cool cats and kitties across Pittsburgh might still be laughing to this day. I know I do every time I think of it.

Here's a tip, friends. Humility is a wonderful thing. More people should try it—especially those running for high political office (ahem, ahem). 'Tis a far, far better thing to underpromise and over-deliver, instead of taking the opposite approach.

They say pride goeth before the fall. Or, in this case, before *two* gutter balls. Just ask Tony from Munhall, who learned it the hard way. On live television. Not cool.

Pap and Circumstance

Jim had heard his parents argue before, so this time didn't faze him much. Something about picking up the wrong yogurt at the store, which then escalated into "You never listen to me," which then leapt higher to "If you said anything worth listening to, then I might listen better," and so on, until a heavy silence fell and the aw-shucks apologies came that returned everything to an even keel again.

Except this time, the escalations kept escalating. Voices became louder and higher-pitched. Lines began to get crossed into virgin and scarier emotional territory. The silence eventually fell but wasn't heavy this time. Instead, in its wake, the air felt electric, alive, pregnant with still-untapped verbal energy that could explode like a spark in an oxygen tank any second.

Not the best time to be preparing for one's high school graduation ceremony, thought Jim. The class of 1976. The Fighting Bisons. Or, this year only, the Fighting Bison-Tennials.

A popular student, leader of the marching band, president of the Kiwanis Club, and member of student council, Jim had also been voted by his peers to speak at commencement. The event had been scheduled for the city's main sports arena, a structure that Jim's Pap had helped to build some fifty years earlier. Such a large venue became necessary, thanks to the enormous number of seniors. The ceremony began at 7 p.m. Graduates needed to be in the staging area behind the draping by 6:15. The kitchen clock now read 5:55. Time to go.

With a big speech ahead of him in front of thousands of people, Jim felt the need to relieve himself. Urgently. While Jim fumbled with the slippery graduation gown and started taking care of his bathroom business, his dad grabbed the car keys and headed out the front door to the driveway, mumbling something about letting Momma drive her Momma's Boy to graduation.

At the same time, his mom clicked her high heels through the kitchen into the garage, muttering that if he's so smart, then he could drive Jim to the commencement.

Who knows how these things happen, but Jim, mortarboard slightly askew, emerged from the toilet and found himself alone, with no way to be a passenger to his own rite of passage. He had not learned to drive at sixteen, living in the city with access to public transportation and a cadre of friends, all of whom drove him anywhere he needed to go. But tonight all of those friends already had driven and parked at the arena—to graduate, like him. Or, perhaps, not like him.

"Well, looks like you're in a real pickle there, boy," came a small, wispy sound from the top of the stairs. Jim's eighty-four-year-old Pap. "Heh, heh. Those two really outdid themselves this time, didn't they?"

"Yeah, Pap. I guess they did. What am I gonna do? I have to get to graduation. I have to give a speech! It's after six now, and I can't catch a bus or call a cab that would get me there in time."

"We'll get you there in time, and you'll give your little speech, Jimmy Boy. No worries."

And then the picture emerged in his mind's eye, a picture of both deliverance and dread. Pap would roll his '64 station wagon out from behind the garage—a car that had not been driven in six years—and get Jim there himself.

Listening to Pap try to turn the engine over—a noise that sounded like bagpipes being punched—Jim started wondering what he'd tell his friends. They'd never believe the truth, so he'd have to invent some even wilder story. While squeezing the creative juices from his brain, he heard the station wagon rumble to wheezy life, followed by a reedy "Yee-hoo!" from Pap.

Meanwhile, inside the arena, Jim's folks sat and listened to the elegant strains of "Pomp and Circumstance" as the graduating students filed in. Scanning faces for Jim, neither one could spot him. To be fair, there had to be five hundred kids down there, but soon came the realization of five hundred minus one. The senior class had been shorted one Jim.

Panicked, then shocked, then mortified, they simultaneously cried to each other, "I thought *you* brought him!" They ran out to the lobby, found a pay phone, and called the house—just in time to miss Jim and Pap begin their rickety route-by-station wagon to Downtown.

Later that night, back home, after sharing drinks and snacks with Jim and his fellow graduates, they recounted the story of how Pap's rambling wreck—plugging bumpily along, chugging weird blue fumes from the exhaust, and fiercely hugging the right lane as semis and cars blasted past them—finally made it to the arena, parking acres away from the main doors.

Then, after realizing those doors had been locked once the event began, Pap drew on his knowledge of the building he helped build— sneaking Jim and himself into a service door beneath the main floor. Snaking their way around pumps and pipes and valves and clouds of hot steam, Pap and Jim finally emerged—just as the emcee prepared to introduce Jim for his big speech.

With grease streaks across his gown, and his battered cap barely clinging to his matted-down, steam-flattened hair, Jim walked from the far corner of the arena floor up onto the dais to at-first stunned, then growing, whoops of applause and cheers. He fished his crumpled prepared remarks from inside his gown, looked at them for a second, and let them fall.

Instead, he leaned his elbow on the podium, cocked his head to the side, found his humiliated parents in the sea of seats, leaned into the microphone, and simply said, "Fellow Bison-Tennials, I have one word of advice that I hope you remember the rest of your lives. Then I'm going to finally take my rightful seat. Ready? Here it is. Never leave the house without checking the damn toilet."

And from the darkness behind the platform, Jim could hear a chuckling "Yee-hoo!"

Thank You, Colonel Burnham

Among the back pages of a magazine many years ago, shortly after the end of the Vietnam War, a small ad caught my eye: "POW bracelets available. Let them know you haven't forgotten them."

For a nominal fee, I sent in the form and a few weeks later received my prisoner-of-war bracelet, a thin, bendable silver strip with the name "Col. Mason Burnham" engraved on it, along with the date he went missing in Vietnam. I squeezed the bracelet around my right wrist and wore that silver talisman through all of my middle school and part of my high school years.

Fast-forward about ten years. I found myself in Washington, D.C., attending a professional-development seminar. With most of one afternoon free, I decided to walk around the capital. After walking past the White House and the Washington Monument, I kept on and reached the National Mall. The Lincoln Memorial was in view, and I meant to make my way there but was interrupted by what was then a relatively new feature on that beautiful expanse, the Vietnam Memorial.

Carved into the earth in a V shape, the Vietnam Memorial remains stunning in its simple, yet emotionally powerful presentation of the thousands upon thousands of names—Americans who lost their lives in that Southeast Asian conflict. Visitors start at either end of the V and descend to the vortex, passing row after row of names etched into the black marble.

As I reached the site, the memory of my teenage POW bracelet shot to the front of my brain. Could Colonel Burnham's name be among this tragic compendium? I searched the directory at the entrance to the memorial hoping I wouldn't find that name. But there it was. Col. Mason Burnham. A fallen American hero.

The directory gave the position of each name on the wall, so I carefully descended into the silence of the massive marble V and eventually located the name.

Obviously I had never met the man. I was just a kid when he was captured. All I knew about Vietnam was what I saw on TV each night behind Walter Cronkite's head, where there was an American flag with a number under it—the total number of GIs killed that day.

All I knew was that nightly image, plus the tenuous connection of my POW bracelet. Even as I wore that bracelet every day, I wondered and worried about Colonel Burnham because he was a prisoner of war, not yet a casualty of war. There was always a glimmer of hope. Someday he would be released and sent back home, wherever in the United States that happened to be.

But as I stared up at that unmistakable, unyielding, unalterable carving in that silent wall of black, the hope I recalled from my teenager's consciousness was swept away like so many dried leaves in the wind. And I cried for a moment for Colonel Burnham, his family, his friends, and the life he sacrificed for you and me and every American.

I had a lot of fun this Memorial Day. Went swimming, cooked out a great meal for my family, watched a ball game on TV. And there's nothing wrong about any of that. We're free to do those things, to make our own way in life, and to reap the innumerable benefits of living in this amazing nation.

Yet I also took a moment to think about the man whose name I walked around with on my wrist during some of the most formative years of my life. And I said a silent thank-you to all of those who gave all—for us all.

Thank you, Colonel Burnham. Mission accomplished. Well done. Take your rest.

Shark-Tanked

The motion picture, it has been said, represents the pinnacle of mankind's ability to tell a story.

Not all movies live up to that noble description, naturally. The entire unfortunate *Porky's* series races to mind, for example. But when a strong story meets a gifted director, supported by talented actors, musicians, and technicians, the results can indeed take your breath away.

I've never much cared for the scare genre of films, with one exception. It was the first movie that truly frightened me right out of my wits. You probably had the same reaction the first time you saw it on the big screen.

Jaws.

For those old enough to recall, *Jaws* came out during the middle of 1975 and became the first true summer blockbuster movie. Lines snaked around the block to see this picture. It burgeoned into a phenomenon. The mechanical shark and the John Williams music have since become a bit cliché, but when *Jaws* first emerged, you couldn't avoid it. No one had ever seen anything like it.

I can recall going into downtown Pittsburgh with a couple of high school buddies to see *Jaws* at the great old Warner Theater, a huge auditorium with a superwide screen. When you wanted to really experience a movie in a big way, you bought your ticket at the Warner. And did I ever experience this movie in a big way.

Plus, I had a little help that I hadn't anticipated. More on that in a moment.

My friends and I finally made it to the box office, bought our tickets, walked up the ornate, red-carpeted lobby, made a quick stop at the refreshment counter for some Snow-Caps candy, and entered the theater. Despite the size of the Warner, our showing had nearly sold out. We were lucky enough to find three seats together, but unlucky enough that they were about four rows from the monstrous curved screen. Imax before there was Imax!

I walked into the row first and took my seat beside a woman who was perhaps a little on the heavy side and who shall be known here as Movie Lady.

The feature started, and every eyeball in that darkened auditorium instantly became riveted on the images up on the screen. In the opening of the film, a young female swimmer goes out for nighttime skinny-dip in the ocean, unaware of the ferocity soon to befall her.

Of course, no one in the audience knew what was coming, either. When the shark attack began, I got startled plenty by what I saw—but even more by what I felt.

Movie Lady, next to me, screamed her head off, lifting me about a foot out of my seat, and then at the same time she waved around a big scarf, which was scraping all over my face! 3-D before there was 3-D!

This happened every time that damn shark turned up. You'd hear that cello music start building—dum-DUM-dum-DUM-dum-DUM-dum-DUM—and knew something bad was about to happen, but I had to keep track of *two* scary sources: the shark and Movie Lady.

"Aaaaah!" she'd shriek, and here'd come the scarf again! I missed half the movie thrashing my way out from under that stupid thing. By the moment near the end of the film when the shark crashes onto the boat and starts chomping on the captain, my nerves were beyond shot.

As the movie ended and the lights came up, the audience applauded like mad. I turned to my buddies, and we started to talk about how much we liked it. Just then, I felt a forceful tap on my shoulder from behind and jumped out of my seat. Again. The shark had snuck up behind me! But no, it was only my overly expressive theater neighbor.

"Young man!" Movie Lady shouted. "I just love these types of movies, don't you?"

Time-Warp Saturday

March 16—a date that forever will be known, at least in my head, as Time-Warp Saturday and a day that I'll always remember fondly. Maybe because it fell between the Ides of March and St. Patrick's Day, March 16 a few years ago had something ethereal, magical, wondrous about it. Here's what I mean.

While checking Facebook in the morning, I came across an entry from a guy I knew in high school. Fellow members of the drum section, we marched alongside each other in parades and in halftime shows at the home football games. He played the cymbals in the marching band, and I played the tri-toms. He had posted a You Tube clip from a year or so before, featuring our old band director, who could be seen leading a group of inner-city kids at an area junior high school.

Three seconds into this clip and I was back in the band room watching Mr. B. lead us, his baton twitching, his facial expressions contorting, his torso bouncing to the beat. He had to be in his seventies by then, but he looked as spry and energetic as ever. It felt great to see him at work doing the thing he loved most of all, all over again.

The band room quickly became the place of sanctuary and fantastic friendship in high school, not only for me but for scores—hundreds, in fact—of kids who played for Mr. B. over the many years he taught there. For me, he stood head and shoulders above all other teachers for earning my respect, instilling a desire to meet his expectations, and providing a place where it was always safe to be yourself. Plus, he was primarily a drummer, so the feeling of shared connections between and Mr. B. and me might have actually been stronger than I had with a lot of the other kids. At least that's how it felt to me then, and even today.

Later in the day on that Time-Warp Saturday, my wife and I went to our local high school to see the annual musical, this edition being the old standard *Guys and Dolls*. At dinner I was talking about the fact that my high school did that same show when I was a senior, but I didn't think much more about it.

Until the curtain went up and the 2013 edition of the play started.

Immediately I remembered every lyric and most of the lines, but more than anything else, I saw my old friends in the same roles from three-plus decades ago. The play hadn't changed, of course. The songs sounded the same. The dance numbers were a pretty close approximation of what our school did way back when.

But the sensation of being back there, as my friends turned into Sky Masterson, Nathan Detroit, Sarah Brown, Miss Adelaide, and the rest of the gamblers and missionaries, somehow made the play even more enjoyable as the bunch of sixteen- and seventeen-year-olds carried it off in style this time. A great evening all around.

Karma threw me a curve on Time-Warp Saturday but such a nice one. If nothing else, it reinforced something I've come to realize more and more as each year goes by.

A great teacher will always remain a great teacher. A great collaboration will always remain a great collaboration. And a great life will always remain a great life. So many things to treasure if you just take the time to think about them. Count your blessings, everybody. When you do, you'll find that they're innumerable.

Newsprint and Maple Syrup

One of the best experiences of high school never took place in our high school.

It would happen four times each academic year, seventy-five miles away from the high school building, when a bunch of students working on the school newspaper would pile into one car and drive to the tiny headquarters of a rural weekly to spend the day.

I never got it straight in my mind why this peculiar arrangement had been concocted. The assumption was that this little town's publisher would make a few bucks, but how our faculty adviser ever found this place remained beyond my detective ability.

We attended Carrick High School, part of the Pittsburgh Public Schools system. Our school newspaper was named *The Carrickulum*. I know, clever, right? Our sojourn took us to the offices of *The Meyersdale Republican* in the heart of that quaint borough tucked in a faraway corner of bucolic Somerset County, Pennsylvania.

Believe it or not, besides a carful of kids from Carrick showing up every couple of months to liven up the place, Meyersdale also became known as the Maple Syrup Capital of Pennsylvania, with its annual Maple Festival that draws tourists—seriously—from far and wide. In college, in fact, my wife had a roommate who had been crowned the Maple Queen one year in Meyersdale. Heady stuff, and high praise indeed.

With each visit—after securing clearances from the teachers whose classes we'd be missing that day—this jolly caravan of budding journalists would drive the ninety minutes south, arrive at the paper, pencil out each page's stories for that issue of *The Carrickulum* on layout sheets, and then the real fun started.

In Meyersdale, Pennsylvania, in the mid-'70s, computers remained in the realm of cheesy science-fiction movies playing down at the Bijou. Real people—real newspaper people—instead used these hulking, cast-iron behemoths known as Linotype machines. We would retype all of the approved article copy we had brought with us while listening to the great Linotype lining up the words in order, filling the ancient production room with clinks and clanks.

We'd write the headlines in larger type, with the Linotype assembling all of this inside a wooden frame containing thousands of tiny chunks of raised letters on metal for each page. Photos got sized by hand to fit their available spaces and then were transferred to a series of microscopic dots in reproduction. Once each page—each box—had been proofread by two people, we tightened the box so that nothing fell out or got misplaced and then fit the box into another large cast-iron machine to be inked and printed on newsprint.

It took hours to complete this process for an eight-page newspaper, but we did it and loved every second of it. There were few moments for me as satisfying as picking up a finished, flawless newspaper that you personally helped to write, assemble, and print.

At the *Republican*, a couple of old hands hung around to help us figure things out, but mostly to make sure we didn't destroy their irreplaceable equipment. Those machines had been around, probably, since the turn of the century. In between their smokes, those guys couldn't let a bunch of city punks from Pittsburgh do anything too stupid to their printing house.

The rides to and from Meyersdale had a few interesting occurrences. One time, driving down a lonely two-lane blacktop out in the country, somebody saw a deer not far from the road. Having grown up in the city, we hadn't seen a deer since—well, none of us had ever seen a deer at all, actually. And here one stood, looking at us, standing perfectly still, as if to say, "Yes, please come over and be my friend."

What a bunch of mooks we were. A couple of the girls walked up to the animal to pet it, confident that they would be met with gentleness and affection. But when they got within two feet, the deer grunted, stomped its front hooves, and ran like lightning away from us—all within a second and a half. The girls shrieked, the guys froze, and we all stumbled over and pushed each other out of the way—just like in the *Scooby-Doo* cartoons—to get back in that car.

Then came the time that the guy driving his dad's car for the trip stubbornly left Meyersdale in the wrong direction—despite the rest of us telling him so—and kept going until we saw a sign across the roadway reading, *Welcome to West Virginia!* Mortified, he turned the car around. Twenty minutes later, we ran out of gas. And none of us had any money.

Somehow we made it home from that trip and all the others. Each one loaded with its own stories, adventures, frustrations, and friendships. It lit the flame for me to pursue a life in journalism that still burns today, nearly forty years later, as a professional writer.

The Maple Festival is coming up pretty soon in good old Meyersdale. Maybe I'll wend my way down there to see the old Linotype and tap a tree or two. Making a run at Maple King is not out of the question, either.

Bess and The Fishbowl

T he summers can be interesting, to say the least. Educational,
even.

There's incredible pressure, first of all, to find a job—then
rouse yourself out of bed in time to get to work, deal with the assort-
ment of personalities there, and not burn through your paycheck
on pizza and movies and gasoline and girlfriends so that you have
enough left in your checking account to cover the gouging you're in
for at college to buy your exorbitantly expensive textbooks.

I had my share of weird and wacky summer jobs back then,
but the weirdest and wackiest had to be the summer I spent in The
Fishbowl.

Tucked into an otherwise forgotten and misbegotten corner of
what used to be called the Pittsburgh Press Building, and otherwise
known as the circulation complaint department, The Fishbowl har-
bored a collection of lifetime workers year round and a couple of
sacrificial students each summer. How on earth I ended up there, I
couldn't tell you. But it was a job, so I took it.

In the days before personal computers or laptops, workers inside
The Fishbowl sat on either side of two eight-foot tables. We each had
a telephone, a pad of paper, and a pen. Thick White Pages phone-
books sat within reach, and on smaller tables along the back wall
rested two printed copies of a huge city directory, where you could
locate an address in a number of ways.

But ringed around this entire work environment, this hard-boiled habitat of humanity, stood floor-to-ceiling clear plastic panels. Hence, The Fishbowl.

Most of the lifers working there were older ladies, hard-bitten, cynical, worn down by years of irate newspaper customers screaming through the phone lines about some stupid kid who missed delivering their paper that day, or threw it on the roof or in a puddle or through their front window. My term in The Fishbowl lasted only about twelve weeks, and the ways a newspaper delivery could be screwed up astounded even me.

Our boss—a man I never saw actually enter The Fishbowl (my guess being this particular honor had been tacked onto whatever his real job was)—said we had only one rule. If a customer swore at us, we could hang up. Otherwise they could verbally pummel away, and we had to remain professional and courteous at all times, doing everything we could to get them their daily freaking newspaper.

Yeah, okay, Boss. Easier said than done. We're suffering in this hotbox—and this also was back in the day when people could smoke their heads off inside, and this gang took full advantage of that perk—while you're sitting fat and happy in your little air-conditioned office with no supremely honked-off housewife from McKees Rocks screaming in your ear that she couldn't read her horoscope today.

Actually, for as crusty as those older ladies appeared, most of them treated me and the other young'uns pretty well that summer. One lady in particular. Bess had a kind heart but a serious alcohol problem. When I arrived for work, I usually had to take the last empty seat, the one next to Bess. It didn't take long to understand why. The scent of liquor on her breath became distracting and disconcerting. But again, Bess never drank at work and always treated her coworkers and her callers with respect and patience.

We occasionally worked weekends, so one week I had taken a regular weekday off. As I reported to The Fishbowl the next morning, two seats remained empty. I took one of them and asked if Bess had taken vacation. No, I was told. Bess had been fired the previous day. Seemed her problem had gotten the better of her, and when a caller had become irate and abusive, Bess fired back in similar fashion—and then some. The caller reported her to our boss, and shortly thereafter, he let Bess go.

I learned a lot that summer about workplace dynamics, about controlling my temper, about being patient with people—some of whom just need somebody to talk with, even if it's to complain about a silly newspaper delivery. But the most important lesson came from Bess, who fought her own personal demon as best she could, until one day the demon won and everything changed.

And the lesson is this. If you need help, or if you know of someone who needs help, please get it. It's not a sign of weakness. It's a sign of amazing courage and enormous personal strength. It's a sign that you think enough of your own worth to want to be strong, happy, healthy, and well.

I never learned what happened to Bess. But I sure hope she got the help she needed.

Just You Wait

Late summer in the late '70s. High school band camp, at a wooded facility atop the Laurel Highlands of southwestern Pennsylvania. Everyone had hiked to the very peak of the mountain hosting our weeklong retreat one warm, humid evening for a bonfire and cookout.

Way back when, the marching band at my school numbered well above two hundred students, counting musicians, majorettes, color guard, pom-pom squad, and equipment managers. Add a full team of adults, with the band director and his wife, chaperones for the dorms, and a small contingency from the camp's own staff, and that mountaintop got a little crowded.

My best friend and I, unwilling to wrangle our way to the front of the gaggle of people trying to roast wieners close to the blazing fire, just grabbed a couple of hot dogs apiece and walked over to the perimeter for our meal. Didn't even worry about a bun. Tough guys, you know how it is.

"I think hot dogs are made out of the same stuff as baloney," my buddy declared. "This will be just like eating lunch meat out of the fridge."

"Yeah," came the ill-informed yet affirmative reply. Spectacularly mutual ignorance about to be exposed.

We each took a bite of our respective raw hot dogs, looked each other in the eye in panic and disgust, and spit the mouthful of awfulness into the grass.

"I thought you said that would taste just like baloney!"

"What do I know? You're the stupid one who listened to me!" Couldn't really argue that point now, could I?

As a result, by the time we pushed and wriggled our way back into the food and fire mob, everything had been pretty much roasted and eaten. So it was back down the hill on an empty stomach, with a long night of rumbles and recriminations ahead of us.

And all because of a galling abundance of pretense and a serious lack of patience.

"The strongest of all warriors are these two: time and patience."—Leo Tolstoy.

"Patience is bitter, but its fruit is sweet."—Aristotle.

"Patience is a conquering virtue."—Geoffrey Chaucer.

"He that can have patience can have what he will."—Benjamin Franklin.

Not a bad collection of minds there, all extolling the importance—the fundamental criticality, actually—of patience. This lesson takes a long time to fully sink in. It requires patience to acquire patience. A stunning life fact now that I think about it.

I'd much rather sit and wait for a pizza, freshly made and baked inside a coal-fired brick oven, with a thin crust, super crunchy, and sizzling mozzarella and toppings, than try to chew my way through a soggy, limp leftover slice nuked unevenly in a microwave. That might be way faster, but as pizza goes, it really sucks.

Along the way in my career, I've worked for people who stormed into the office each morning shouting orders, lighting fires under slow movers, leaving fluttering papers and battered people in their wake. They sure got a lot done, but whether everything that got done added value, hit the mark, or made sense sometimes came into question. That's the school of "It's easier to ask forgiveness than permission," and there's a time and place for that.

I've also worked under supervisors whose attitude to managing issues and team members seemed to be summed up as, "Give any problem enough time to sit and stew unattended, and eventually it will just go away." But that's having way too much patience if you ask me.

My experience tells me that occasionally an issue demands immediate, pull-the-emergency-lever, all-hands-on-deck attention. But very occasionally. Most often, if you take the time to think a situation through, trust other people to come through on their end, and act when appropriate, most issues get resolved peacefully and to a satisfactory conclusion. All it takes is patience. If you can wait long enough to get it, that is.

Remember that the next time you're tempted to bypass a fire-roasted weenie. Nearly forty years later, I can still taste that nasty, cold, raw mess. My mountaintop epiphany. Yeah, cook the hot dog. It's worth the wait.

Matchstick Memories

The room sat in near-complete darkness, except for a bright cone of light directly above the workshop space where Adlai sat, hunched, special magnifier goggles strapped to his head, tiny tools in his hands, making repairs to a miniature rolltop desk the size of a salt shaker.

The tiny piece of furniture actually worked, the wooden slats moving up and down to cover or expose the desktop surface. It represented just one of scores of miniature pieces that Adlai had acquired or built himself over the years—a passion born more than four decades earlier.

His repairs finished, Adlai carefully lifted the little rolltop, carried it across his second-floor apartment, and placed it inside the tiny office of one of his display home models, resting on a buffet in his modest dining room.

———◆———

Ava sat on the other side of his freshman English classroom, stunningly beautiful with a winning smile. Her questions and comments in class demonstrated an impressive intellect, as well. Adlai came from a small-town high school shy and unsure. College offered a fresh start, a clean break, a way to find and build a new life. But all he could think of was Ava. So he started writing her letters, sitting at the rolltop desk his mother insisted he bring to his dorm room—a piece of home, a thousand miles and a lifetime away.

———

As he placed the tiny desk in its place, Adlai looked at his collection of miniatures and decided to give them a good dusting and polishing. The hat stand, the love seat, everything could use a little attention. He didn't mind. It gave him something productive to do. It had been a whole week since he dusted and polished his pint-size gallery, after all.

———

After a week of letters, Adlai finally mustered the courage to approach Ava following English class. She acknowledged receiving his letters but asked that he wait until midterms had passed to go on a date. He respected that and looked forward to dinner. They began going out, sporadically at first, but by their junior year were a couple. Adlai had an off-campus apartment by then. He took extra care to help Ava with her coat and hat, hanging them on the hat stand and then joining her on the love seat, where—well ...

———

In the miniature dining room, with the two place settings resting in perfect symmetry on the tabletop, Adlai stopped dead in his tracks. He stared at the little room, his breathing shallow, his hands perspiring. "This room might look clean and pristine and perfect," he thought to himself, "but I know better."

———

As graduation approached, Adlai prepared to propose. Ava brought such happiness to his life that he wanted it to be that way forever. He planned the big moment for a Saturday evening. He would prepare her favorite dish, they would enjoy a wonderful meal together, and then he would escort her to the love seat and ask for her hand. He had transformed that bare-bones, off-campus kitchen into a culinary symphony fit for a four-star chef, the aromas and steam filling the apartment as seductively as the question he planned to ask later that night.

———◆———

Still held in a frozen stare, Adlai looked at the tiny little telephone on the tiny little end table. He thought he even heard it ringing, ringing, ringing …

———◆———

The phone rang as Adlai cooked their dinner. He ran into the next room to pick up the receiver. Ava was on the other end. Seems an old friend— an old boyfriend, actually—had come to visit from her home back in New York. His family owned a large company that collected, shipped, and sold barges full of junk and scrap metal up and down the East River. He would be graduating the same time as Ava and had a big job lined up with his father. He'd run the company within ten years. And he wanted her to come home with him. He would give her a happy, loving, comfortable life. And she said yes. She felt terrible about this; Adlai had been so good to her all through college, but she had to think long term. She said she loved Adlai, and wished him a happy life, and said good-bye, and hung up the phone. That was forty-six years ago.

———◆———

Adlai rousted himself from his temporary stupor. He felt as though he was seeing his collection of miniatures with fresh eyes for the first time in a long time. Yes, they were lovely. Yes, they were special. Yes, they captured a time and a life that had once been very real and very good.

And yes, they had to go. Now. Today. After nearly a half-century of wasted retrospection, these little pieces of matchstick memories had outlived their usefulness and purpose. It hurt too much to have these little reminders of lost happiness puncturing his heart. If a degree in English, and a career teaching English in middle school, taught him nothing else, it taught Adlai that after you've suffered enough, for God's sake, pick yourself up and get moving again.

He thought about putting the miniatures on eBay and making a few bucks, but that didn't feel right. His birthday was coming up soon, though, so he decided to give himself an early present and just pitch the whole collection right into the Dumpster behind his apartment building. The same apartment he'd had since moving off-campus all those years ago.

As he carried the model across the back parking lot on the way to the Dumpster, he took one last look. The front door, with its three little diamond-shaped windows facing outward. So lovely ...

———◆———

Nine in the evening. The doorbell rang. Adlai, startled, peered through the peephole to see who would be calling at this late hour. He opened the door and saw a sixty-seven-year-old woman, who had married young, taken a lot of abuse from a wealthy alcoholic husband, had two children who both moved far from home, lived very comfortably but very unhappily, got divorced, and who had always regretted the one that got away: the just-scraping-by, middle school English teacher, standing slack-jawed in the doorway.

———◆———

Ava. Ava came back. The miniatures disappeared, and Ava arrived. Happy birthday, Adlai.

Mrs. H. and the Sanctity of the News

She stood five foot two, maybe. Weighed a hundred pounds sopping wet. But, boy oh boy, you didn't want to cross her or let her down.

Mrs. H., our high school newspaper faculty adviser, took that role seriously and expected us to do the same. Even though we were printing only four editions of the school paper each academic year, she held us to the highest ethical standards of fact-finding, sourcing our stories properly, telling each side of a story factually, making sure all names carried the proper spelling, performing quality layout of the pages, and representing ourselves with dignity and pride as reporters and editors.

If any student was found to have misrepresented a source or, worse, fabricated "facts" in an article, the repercussions could be heard up and down the full length of our school's corridors. Lockers rattled. Lights flickered. Bladders strained.

Mrs. H. might have been tiny in stature, but she remained a titanic force. A bastion, a beacon, a touchstone of character and unquestioned ethics. And it rubbed off on me, especially as a student who planned to major in journalism in college and as editor in chief of that selfsame high school newspaper.

All of which flashed to the front of my mind as allegations—since proved true—arose concerning *NBC Nightly News* anchor Brian

Williams. It seems Williams's story about riding in a U.S. military helicopter that came under enemy fire during the Iraq invasion in 2003 was a fabrication. He did ride on an American military helicopter, but it never attracted enemy fire. *Stars and Stripes*, the armed forces publication, exposed the exaggerated version of the story promoted by Williams for more than a decade. Since that revelation, more charges of false reporting by Williams have arisen concerning coverage of Hurricane Katrina.

NBC News has launched an internal investigation to determine what happened in these instances and has promised to communicate its findings. But the horse has long vacated the barn at this point, guys.

Did Williams embellish his helicopter adventure just once, and the lie accelerated away and out of his control? Did he, as he insists, simply "misremember" being shot at? Did he feel compelled to pump up his credentials as a field reporter and simply get carried away?

My theory goes like this: Journalism, in its truest, highest, and most ethical form, is the exception and not the rule today. With so many ways to communicate, everyone can be a "journalist." True, properly trained, professional journalists find themselves in the minority and might see their standards slide, just to keep up. I think Williams fell victim to this sad truth.

Beyond the competition from twenty-four-hour cable news, instant news via Twitter, and other outlets nipping at the networks' heels, just look at Williams's own personal record. He has regularly appeared on late-night talk shows, yukking it up with the hosts. He "slow-jams" the news (whatever that means) with Jimmy Fallon on *The Tonight Show*. He has honed his comedic chops, hosting *Saturday Night Live*. He has worked as hard—maybe harder—to become a celebrity as he has to remain a credible journalist. Watching Williams do these things always made my skin crawl, if even just a little bit.

In the course of attaining his celebrity, maintaining ethical standards of quality journalism might have simply fallen by the wayside. Fact-checking? Attributing sources? Balanced reporting? Aw, that's too much work. David Letterman won't think that's cool. Nobody gives you any credit for that boring stuff.

Yeah, not until you drop the ball as spectacularly as Lyin' Brian. Mrs. H. would have kicked his ass up and down the halls of Rockefeller Center. I bet if I called her, maybe she still could.

Reconsidering Holden

I t quickly became the first book I couldn't put down. The one I read over and over again, underlining sentences that I thought were especially funny or pointed or that sounded as if they came straight out of my head.

The Catcher in the Rye, by J.D. Salinger, in twelfth-grade high school advanced English. When it became the first assigned reading during my freshman year in college, as well, I remember writing my high school English teacher to tell him how happy I was.

Holden Caulfield's odyssey from prep school expulsion to a lost three days in New York City, hiding from his parents before sneaking home to say good-bye to his little sister, has served as the baseline description of overwrought adolescent angst since its publication in 1951. And maybe that's the problem I find myself facing today.

For as much as I identified with some, not all, of Holden's cynicism as a teenager and college student, when I read that book today as a husband and father in his mid-fifties, I have to say much of the thrill is gone. Sure, it's still funny in spots, sad in others, but I find I have a lot of trouble identifying with Holden's predicament now.

He constantly dubs adults and peers as "phony," and without a doubt some people truly are. Yet from my perspective today, a lot of that name calling in the book only serves as a way for Holden to avoid his own phoniness, shallowness, inexperience, and immaturity.

He swims in a sloppy, sloshy pool of fantasy and invented adventure. What appealed to me back then as a harmless diversion today instead reads like a harmful delusion. Holden needs to escape to a world of his own making because he can't handle the reality of his own life. A life of failure and confusion, much of it self-inflicted.

My observations might strike you as the grumpy rumblings of a codger-in-training, and maybe they are. But maybe they're also the reflections of a point of view that, by necessity, changes over time. Maybe they're the sound of a mind that's been through enough stuff over the years to appreciate the difference between what's worth worrying about, getting worked up over, and deserving of attention and effort—versus what's simply not.

So much of what troubles Holden on his ever-deepening journey into despair and isolation really shouldn't. His older brother becomes a screenwriter. His father is a corporate attorney. His younger brother dies as a child. His baby sister idolizes him. His old girlfriend is always just a phone call away, but he never makes the call. In one way or another, each of these facts becomes a source of piled-up frustration.

Salinger never wrote a sequel to *The Catcher in the Rye*, but if he had, I would hope that Holden would have eventually learned that assigning value or meaning to one's own life has nothing to do with how others live theirs.

Every day is a choice. Your choice. You can choose to be happy, or not. You can choose to live by faith in a higher power, or not. You can choose to approach other people with an attitude of respect and service, or not. The choice always rests with you.

Holden tells his kid sister, Phoebe, "What I have to do, I have to catch everybody if they start to go over the cliff—I mean if they're running and they don't look where they're going I have to come out from somewhere and catch them. That's all I do all day. I'd just be the catcher in the rye and all. I know it's crazy, but that's the only thing I'd really like to be."

You learn as you get older that Holden's aspirations are not only way too grand, they're ill-advised, not to mention downright impossible. Save yourself first. Choose to be happy. The rest usually takes care of itself.

Trading Eights

M r. B., the band director, pulled the door of the tiny rehearsal room shut and sat at the beyond-beat-up public school piano as I took my place behind a well-worn set of public school drums. My first-ever, sophomore-year audition to make the high school stage band—or jazz band, as some would call it—had arrived, and the rising tide of nerves threatened to capsize my cranium at any moment.

"Get ready, Hayes. We're gonna do some trading eights," Mr. B. shouted.

Trading eights? What in the world is that? The river of panic began cresting its banks. Do I ask him, or will that scuttle my chances before we even get started? Quickly I made the right decision and asked for clarification.

Turns out, trading eights occurs when two musicians take turns playing eight bars of improvisational music. Mr. B. would play eight bars on the piano as I kept time on the drums, and then he would trade it over to me to cover eight bars of drum solo, and back and forth. He wanted to see how well I could handle keeping the beat and then providing some nice flourishes on the drum kit.

He started us off, and it took a couple of go-rounds for me to get truly comfortable, but soon we were trading eights with confidence and skill and enjoyment. Two musicians teaming up and taking turns.

Balance on the one hand and the chance to really challenge yourself on the other. What a great idea.

This principle has crossed my mind many times since those glory days in the high school band room.

Take the handful of job supervisors over the years who operated daily under the erroneous and dangerous belief that their staffs worked for them, not the organization, and who regularly took credit for what went right and passed blame for what went wrong. They never achieved balance, only discord, dissent, and disrespect. Their character—or lack thereof—precluded allowing, much less celebrating, the innovation, initiative, or inspired effort of individuals on their teams, instead creating toxic work environments where no one ever extended an ounce of extra effort.

But then there were those bosses and coworkers—including many CEOs along the way—who understood the importance and essential value of building camaraderie, setting high expectations, providing the tools and encouragement and trust needed to meet those standards, and then guiding and correcting and supporting their people. Trading eights with those folks? I could have operated in that zone all day, and most days did. *Work* became a misnomer in those types of positive settings.

It's not hard to think of examples in which trading eights works great. Try to think of it the next time a coworker needs advice with a task, or has just successfully completed a project. Or the next time one of your kids wants to help dry the dishes or run the sweeper. Or the next time a neighbor needs an extra pair of hands on a project. Show your interest, let them prove their skill, and then celebrate the achievement together.

Or, conversely, think of this principle the next time you're tempted to zoom past a long line of traffic just to wedge your way in at the merge point. Or when mature, reasoned debate gets swept aside in favor of personal insults and crass bullying. Tsk-tsk. For shame. That's not in the spirit of trading eights. That's being a selfish jerk, and I've got to believe people are capable of behaving better than that.

Showing mutual respect, maintaining a healthy and solid balance, and leaving room for individual excellence to shine. Trading eights. It's truly not all that difficult, it's more than worth the effort, and it makes life a little more tolerable and a lot more fun.

So thanks for the lesson, Mr. B. I've never forgotten it and still try to live by it. Don't hit the mark 100 percent of the time but am always shooting for it.

Oh, and by the way, in case you were wondering, I passed the audition that day and made stage band.

Uncle Jim

My Uncle Jim was a bear of a guy, a man's man, and it was impossible not to like him.

He and my aunt had three daughters, and because my mom and aunt were sisters, our family spent a lot of time at their house, and vice versa. I loved them all, but when we got together, there were the two adult women, three female cousins, and my two younger sisters. That's a heck of a lot of estrogen in one place for a budding stud like me. (You can stop giggling now, dear reader.)

So naturally, I tried to hang around my dad and my Uncle Jim as much as possible.

Uncle Jim had a nice job in an office someplace, and he maintained a solid, respectable, middle-class Pittsburgh life for all of his girls. He always had a wide grin to welcome you with and a handshake that I always thought was what it would feel like to shake hands with a grizzly bear, as his great paw would knead my scrawny knuckles against each other. He had a great, deep voice that carried like crazy, and he always had a joke ready for you. Uncle Jim was awesome.

Oh, and one more thing. He had a wooden leg.

The source of mystery and a little bit of wariness on our part as kids, Uncle Jim's wooden leg never slowed him down, never kept him from any activities with his own family or with our very large extended family. He never talked about it, other than to encourage us to give it a knock for good luck every now and then.

I never saw him in pain because of it, never heard him complain about it, never watched him take it off or put it on, never actually saw it at all now that I think about it. His cars were specially adapted so that he could drive to work, drive to family events, drive wherever he wanted, just like anybody else. Uncle Jim's wooden leg was just a part of him. Unusual but accepted. It contributed to what made him such a great uncle, at least in my eyes.

Days, more like hours really, before I was to leave for college, Uncle Jim passed away unexpectedly. A titan of my youth, gone. If college is where you go to grow up, I got a head start on the process. A brutal head start. It remains one of the great regrets of my life that I could not be at Uncle Jim's funeral. It would have been such an honor to serve as one of his pallbearers. But my aunt insisted that I needed to start my college career as planned, so we honored her request.

It's been nearly thirty-five years since I heard Uncle Jim's voice, saw his big smile grinning at me, felt my knuckles getting squeezed in his grip, or gave his wooden leg a knock for good luck. But I think of him a lot, especially every November 11. For Uncle Jim was a veteran of World War II.

He lost his leg after an intense, close-range firefight in Europe. I've never gotten the details of the story perfectly straight, but it happened near a farmhouse where rifle fire was happening with mere feet between the combatants. Uncle Jim was shot in his leg and lost it later, coming home with commendations for valor and a wooden prosthetic.

They call his the Greatest Generation because of what they accomplished, which was nothing less than saving the world from totalitarianism. But also because of how they did it, and the fact that they came back and just got on with building their families, careers, and communities. I don't know the details of how he lost his leg because Uncle Jim never talked about it. That chapter was closed. It became more important to love his wife and daughters, and to keep a little nephew company as we sat in his backyard and listened to Bob Prince call a Pirates game on the radio.

Heroes like Uncle Jim are everywhere. They might not talk about it much, and that's their prerogative. But on this, and every, Veterans Day, it's our time to talk, to thank them for their service and their sacrifice.

So thanks, Uncle Jim. I'll never forget you. Knock, knock.

The Long Climb Back

Every now and then, when business takes me over that way, I make a slight detour and drive through the neighborhood where I grew up. Sometimes it makes me smile, but more often it pesters my mind and hurts my heart.

Because, you see, the old neighborhood looks just that – old. Tired. A little beat-up by life, and age, and an encroaching sense of decline. It also looks a lot smaller and the houses squeezed a lot tighter together than I remember.

Maybe it's something that a fresh coat of paint on the front porch awnings could help remedy, but I fear the trouble goes deeper than that. Driving down the street, rattling off the names of each family in every house I passed, I wondered if any still lived there. It seemed unlikely.

Recalling the hours spent playing and riding bikes with friends in the front street, or in the alley behind our house, or in the open field behind the houses across the street, I wondered if the kids living there now did the same. For whatever reason, that seemed just as unlikely.

Now, please understand, all of these observations come as the result of a 30-second car ride, so the chances of me being completely wrong remain fairly high. And I hope I am wrong, because I could not have asked for a happier, safer, more loving and support-based childhood, growing up where I did. My fondest wish would be for every kid to have the kind of family and neighbors – in the truest sense of the word, where we looked out for each other with shared concern and support – that my sisters, friends, and I had.

The impression these days, however, draws a somewhat dimmer view. But there is hope. Tangible, tactical hope, that the old girl can make the long climb back to prosperity and pride. The first glimpse came in a brief newspaper article describing how a young couple recently purchased a long-established bar and grill, and converted it into a friendly neighborhood bistro.

The story placed this effort into context, saying that, "For every Lawrenceville, East Liberty, South Side or Downtown that's been the apple of developers' eyes, there are dozens of other struggling neighborhoods like Mount Oliver that have never fully recovered in post-steel Pittsburgh...With a business corridor with great bones, new leadership and activity in an organized neighborhood group and a planned urban farm, the (bistro owners) may be buying in early on an area poised for a turnaround. Here's hoping more will do the same."

We're knee-deep into the season of gift-giving, thanks-giving, and second chance-giving. The season of rethinking, rebirth, and renewal. The risk that this couple has taken on, in attempting to plant a flag of confidence and belief in the potential of my old stomping grounds to start over, is not only admirable, but worthy of applause. And action.

It took 30 seconds in a car to create a discouraging mental image. It took 30 seconds to read a story in the paper that created a mental image of hope and fortitude. At some point during this holiday season, I plan to punch my ticket on behalf of and in appreciation of the place where I grew up, and eat a meal in that new neighborhood bistro.

I'm betting the long climb back could start with a beer, a hamburger, a grateful respect for a neighborhood's wonderful legacy, and a healthy dose of faith in its future. It's a bet I'd be so grateful to win.

Conclusion

As a student at St. Joe's School, I learned about blessings. Where they come from, why we receive them, and how much we need to be thankful for them. The experiences of my youth, just a few of which appear in this book, add up to an enormous source of blessings—actually the launchpad to a lifetime of blessings that continues today.

The fact that all of this happened in a tiny place called Mount Oliver—not even one square mile in area—only adds to the amazement. But, on the other hand, maybe the fact that my hometown was so small made all the difference. Maybe houses clumped together, classrooms filled to the brim so that you got to know your classmates like your own sisters and brothers, neighbors who knew and looked after each other's kids and houses, familiar sights and sounds and people you saw just about every day—maybe those considerations jumbled together created the secret sauce after all.

All I know is that the world would be a better, safer, sunnier, funnier, happier place if we all had the chance to Grow Up Giffin.

About the Author

Tim Hayes brings nearly three decades of communications counsel and tactical experience—particularly at the leadership level—to clients. He shares much of that experience and lessons learned along the way in his first book, *Jackass in a Hailstorm: Adventures in Leadership Communication*. In his second book, *Growing Up Giffin: Reflections on a Happy Steeltown Boyhood*, Tim shares stories of his youth as a city kid who, looking out his bedroom window each morning, could see the orange glow of Pittsburgh's booming steel mills on the horizon.

Tim has been selected as the Number 1 Speechwriter by the Washington, D.C., chapter of the International Association of Business Communicators; named winner of the top speech in the nation by *PR News* in its Platinum PR Awards; the recipient of a national Cicero Speechwriting Award; and honored by more than twenty regional and state awards for excellence in writing. He is the subject of two *USA Today* articles, is a regular guest expert on regional and national radio programs, and has become recognized as a national resource regarding helping leaders perfect their public personas.

Since 2000 he has led Tim Hayes Consulting (known officially as Transverse Park Productions LLC) as president, working to effectively position organizations in the marketplace through intelligent, well-reasoned and well-crafted speechwriting, executive message development, employee programs, government-relations support, technical writing, and public relations.

Through his Total Pro line of services, Tim offers personalized leadership communications training, such as presentation skills coaching and media interview preparation tactics, in group settings, management retreats, conference appearances, and one-to-one consulting sessions.

Tim has served leaders of all types of organizations through annual reports, transparency and sustainability reports, strategic speechwriting and presentation coaching, employee communications efforts, and other high-level communications designed to achieve key business objectives.

Tim has worked directly with CEOs and other senior executives of major corporations, including Daimler-Chrysler, United States Steel Corp., H.J. Heinz Co., PNC Financial Services Group Inc., Mellon Financial Corp., Koppers Inc., GNC Inc., PPL Corp., Grant Thornton LLC, Fleet Boston Corp., Highmark Blue Cross Blue Shield, Banco Santander Corp., Federated Investors Inc., Wabtec Inc., Michael Baker Corp., iGate Global Solutions Inc., Universal Stainless & Alloy Products Inc., Allegheny Ludlum Inc., Kennametal Inc., and the Pittsburgh Steelers.

His career began as a newspaper reporter, winning a statewide award for news coverage of his alma mater, Indiana University of Pennsylvania. Tim earned a bachelor's degree in journalism from IUP in 1982.

He and his wife, Ellen, live in suburban Pittsburgh, Pennsylvania. They have three wonderful and accomplished grown children. Tim tries his level best every day, with varying degrees of success, to be a loving husband, devoted father, dutiful son, dependable brother, steadfast friend, and reliable professional consultant.

Learn more about how Tim's services can help you and your organization by visiting www.timothy hayes.com.

Made in the USA
Lexington, KY
09 April 2019